Alchemy of Dreams and Other Poems

Alchemy of Dreams
and Other Poems

Michael Fantina

Hippocampus Press
———————
New York

Acknowledgments:
"Death on the Moor" appeared in *Literary Hatchet* No. 12 (2015).
"The Sorceress at the End of Space-Time" appeared in *Startling Space Stories* #3 (2012).
"Sea Spell in Winter" appeared in *This Haunted Sea* (Rainfall Chapbooks, 2010).
"Conversion" appeared in *Lyric* (2011).

Copyright © 2017 by Michael Fantina
Cover painting and interior artwork copyright © 2017 by Steve Lines
Cover design, background, and lettering by Kevin I. Slaughter.
All Rights Reserved.

No part of this work may be reproduced in any form or by any means without the written permission of the publisher.

Published by Hippocampus Press
P.O. Box 641, New York, NY 10156.
http://www.hippocampuspress.com

Hippocampus Press logo designed by Anastasia Damianakos.

First Edition
1 3 5 7 9 8 6 4 2

ISBN13: 978-1-61498-168-8

Contents

Vanished Realms and Lost Worlds 13

    A Dream of the Minotaur 15
    Genius Loci 16
    Spirits 18
    Roc 19
    Cecily 20
    The Haunted Inn 21
    Stone Pillars 23
    The Haunted Archipelago 24
    When Wizards Meet 26
    Lyonnesse 26
    A Careless Kiss 27
    A Dream of Gold 28
    A Centauress 29
    On Wings of Steel 30
    The Dawn 31
    The Return 31
    Angels of Ice 32
    Cockaigne 33
    The Pale Château 35
    Nymphs 36
    I Circle Methane Seas 39
    The Lover's Curse 39
    I Wander 41
    The Satrap 42
    My Dreams Take Me 42
    The Ghost Army 43
    Ride the Night Wind 44
    Dispatched 45
    Out of the Mountain Pool 46
    The Call of Orion 46
    Like a Stone 47
    Girl from Altair 48

Like Solomon	49
Ghost of the Fen	49
Haunted	51
Among the Stars	53
In Nan Modal	53
The Dream Rider	54
Ghost Kings of Mu	55
Atlantis	57
Strange Harbor	58
The Nymph's Prayer	58
The Temptress	62
A Traveler through Time	63
Strange Stars	64
In Isfahan	64
Ganymede	65
Ulysses	65
Intruder	66
Castles in the Air	67
Only an Evil Wind Went Roaring	67
Spirit Cave	68
Vengeful Vipers Vex All This	69
A Vision	69
The Fatal Shore	70
Ur	71
Cold Is the River	72
In Castles of Steel	73
Realm of Dreams	74
Argosy of Dreams	77
Centaur Love	78
Barge	79
Lost World	80
The Glen	82
The Harpy	82
Elemental	85
I Have Danced with Princesses	85
The Haunted Temple	86
The Sorceress at the End of Space-Time	87
The Seneschal	92

The Singing Sword	93
The Witches' Château	97
1934	97
The Forsaken City	98
I Sigh to Orion	100
In Upland Fields	101
The Ghost, the Gold, and the Dark	103

Down to the Sea in Ships 105

Secluded Bays	107
These Haunted Hills I Roam	108
The Drowning	109
Under an Iron Moon	109
The Viking Horn	111
Rendezvous	112
Song of the Sea Dog's Ghost	113
One Misty Morn	114
Beguiled	116
In the Moonlight	116
Iron and Silver	117
Sea Shanty	118
Harold Owen Confronts His Brother's Ghost	119
Leviathan	120
The Matilda	120
Bethany	122
Xardoc Ibrahim	124
A Dark Dream of the Sea	125
Sea Magic	126
The Ferryman	127
The Schooner	128
The Vanished Sea	129
Above the Bay in Rajapore	130
Sea Ghosts and Shipwrecks	131
Mount Carmel by the Sea	132
A Shipman's Dream	133
The Witch of the West	134
Calypso	135
The Dark Girl	136

The Ship 137
Six Days out of Zanzibar 137
Conversion 138
A Dream of Leviathan 139
Bell Isle 140
By the Haunted Sea 140
I Heard Swift Ghostly Fingers 141
The Trysting Place 142
Windward and Lee 144
Seven Sisters 145
Love Uncanny 146
The Sea King's Daughter 150
Arcanum 152
Vengeance for Io 152
The Legs of Leviathan Loop 153
Fugue 155
The Flying Dutchman 156
Flight 19 157
The Merman Tempts a Girl 158
Lovesick 159
Call of the Restless Sea 160
I Wander 160
Sea Dream 161
Merlin's Daughter 163
Veronique 164
A Sea Change 165
A Sea Spell in Winter 167
Lure of the Siren 168

Lovers, Ghosts, and Monsters 169

Vengeance 171
Death on the Moor 173
Stars That Sunder 174
The Wizard Makes a Girl 175
The Lover 176
Idol Found in the Woods 178
The Constant Lover 179
I Ride the Nightmare 180

The Fell at Twilight	182
A Midnight Tryst	183
Wizard Love	184
The Necromancer	186
In Amber	187
The Abandoned Lover	188
Dark Machinations	190
Rolling the Bones	192
Tan Girl	193
She-Wolf	194
Night of the Banshee	195
She Soared Upon the Wind	197
Illicit Rendezvous	197
The Madness of the Moon	199
Withered Roses	199
Forlorn	201
Lycanthropy at Dusk	201
Purchased Love	202
Fable	203
Under These Stars	204
Girl in the Dunes	204
She	205
The Black Comet	206
Ghost Poet	207
Regret	208
Clarice	209
The Love Potion	210
The Princess of Grant Street	211
The Spire and the Ghost	212
Warlocks and Mages	213
Sower of Discord	214
Moon Prayer	216
The Wind	217
Zahlore	218
Ingénue	220
The Muse	221
The Upper Air	221
The Inconstant Lover	222

The Sorcerer Fashions a Lover for Himself 223
The Offering 227
The Pretty Jinn 228
An Encounter at Dusk 230
Three Kisses 231
Sarah Jane 232
Above the Fallen Gate 234
Where Shadows Weave 234
The Ghost of Guinevere 235
Cold Love 235
Haunted Château 236
To Wake the Dead 237
Raquel 238
Moon Love 240
The Ghost Train 241
Aphasia 243
The Fire Fairy 244
All Hallows Eve 245
Phantom Wife 247
Bewitched and Beguiled 249
Gray Eyes 252
Street Walker 253
The Silver Pin 254
The Wicked Girl 255
The Ghost Bell 256
An Iron Gong 257
Dark Paramour 258
Una Sandoval 264
Frankenstein 265
Ghost Rider 266
A Nightmare 268
Selene 269
Lamentation 271
Alchemy of Dreams 273
The Lover Despairs 274
Duplicity 275
The Girl 276
I Dream of Her 276

    Sylph 277
    Like Queen Mab 279
    The Awful Dream 280
    Ghost Wife 282
    Jocelyn 283
    Under the Pole Star 284

A Wellspring of Arcana **287**
    The Centauress 289
    One Misty Morn 289
    The Ale 290
    Daydream at Dusk 291
    The Stuff of Dreams 291
    The Abbey Bells 293
    Moonlight 293
    Vespers 294
    Time and Space 295
    Spoons 296
    The Sunken Road 297
    New Love for Old 297
    Isfahan 298
    Remembrance 299
    Serenity 299
    Scryer 300
    The Glory Hand 300
    The Old Shop 301
    Winter Spells 302
    Girl with a Crystal Ball 303
    Give Me a Brand 304
    The Bell 304
    The Riven Oak 305
    The Rescue 306
    Ransom 307
    Hammer 307
    The End of the Wizards 308
    A Spell in Measure 310
    Magics 310
    Winter 311

Harpies and Ravens	314
Love Is Cruel	315
The Pond	315
Lover of the Moon	316
A Ghost	317
Ghost in the Mirror	317
Wind-Blown Dream	318
The Dusk	319
The Glue	320
The Haunted Clock	320
Nocturnal	321
Of Fairy Rings and Cedar Chests	322
The Woodland Nymph	323
Pursued by the Jinn	325
The Gander	325
An Elixir of Love	327
The Ghostly Monarch	328
The Forsaken City	329
The Moon Riders	330
I Remember	332
With a Vengeance	332
Wizard	333
Men	334
The Harpy Queen	335
A Fragment from a Dream	337
I Dream	337
A Ghost Girl from 1918	340
The Caliph's Lover	341
Pursuit of the Belovèd	342

*Vanished Realms and
Lost Worlds*

A Dream of the Minotaur

A clock with its gear wheels has garnered this grange,
    Near cool and outlandish long streams.
A place where odd nightmares coevally range,
Where the elms are most frightful, outré and strange,
    This place of incredible dreams!

Down canyons where cloisters of clandestine Celts
    Commingle with comely young girls,
The Minotaur rises, his face full of welts,
As the terrified girls all undo their gold belts,
    Replace them with strings of long pearls!

Now I race down that canyon and call to them there,
    And offer them aid for their love.
They handily pledge all their love as I stare
As their warm girlish breath hangs like mist on the air,
    And each as white as a dove!

They fall to their knees and they call me their "lord."
    I draw out my weapon and spin.
I spin toward that beast with my terrible sword,
The Minotaur lays where my steel has him gored,
    As my dreams turn to lust and such sin!

I turn and those girls have arisen and stand,
    And murder there is in their eyes!
Now each is a werewolf with jaws that command

A fealty to all in this hellish dreamland,
    They slay me and I've lost my prize!

They tear me to pieces. They dance on my grave,
    Then turn into girls as before.
They bury me under a thick granite pave,
And then with aloes their pale bodies they lave,
    Then scamper out onto the moor.

A clock with its gear wheels has garnered this grange,
    Near cool and most outlandish streams.
A place where odd nightmares coevally range,
Where the elms are most frightful, outré and strange,
    This place of incredible dreams!

Genius Loci

I'm cast adrift in starry spans
Where comets sail through icy cold,
Where meteors in caravans
Glow with a yellow starry gold.

Cast on a barren planetoid,
Where idols like to huge dragoons
Lurch in this icy midnight void,
Lit by a dozen pockmarked moons.

My ship half sunk into the dust
Of centuries, below a tor,
As red and hard as ancient rust;
Its sides all sheathed in iron ore.

I breathed the thin air with a gasp,
And felt like one accursed, dragooned.
I would survive, to hard life clasp,
On this strange world, alone, marooned.

I made my home within the cleft
Of one huge idol, tilting there.
Then once inside, upon the left,
I found a spiral stone cut stair.

Up, up into the idol's eye,
I climbed to find a spacious room;
I gazed though it with half a sigh,
Gazed on a barren realm of gloom.

I saw vast cities withered there,
With lofty minarets of stone,
And mighty domes in disrepair,
And temples like to none I've known.

Slim towers each like some sharp tine
Rose dizzily into the air,
Some tilt wildly, some supine,
Lay buried in the red dust there.

Then in the distant mountains' shade,
Below a ruined parapet,
Across a flag stone promenade,
Rose up a giant silhouette.

The genius loci of the place
Brought up its arms toward sallow moons,
As dust storms would that view erase
Like monumental dark typhoons.

I'm cast adrift in starry spans
Where comets sail through icy cold,
Where meteors in caravans
Glow with a yellow starry gold.

Spirits

Spirits here
And spirits after
Front and rear
From floor to rafter.

Spirits there
And spirits looming,
In the air,
All men they're dooming.

Spirits sigh
So pale and fragile,
Spirits high,
So grim and agile.

Spirits wan,
And chalk cliffs soaring,
Spirits gone
To combers roaring.

Spirits teem,
And spirits haunting
One dark dream,
With spirits daunting.

Spirit girls
Like one wan willow,
Lovely curls
To hold and pillow.

Spirits fall
Diagonally,
Spirits call
Far out at sea.

Roc

On pylons weathered by grim centuries
I stood alone in arcane winter dreams.
Below me there the twisted, frozen streams,
While I sensed something in the frigid breeze
That swayed the elms and massive chestnut trees,
Below the clouds the distant sunlight gleams
Upon the outstretched wings of that which seems
A titan roc who's flown across these seas.

I gaped in awe, the monstrous bird would ride
The soaring thermals from the distant hills.
I watched its massive bulk so deftly glide;

It gave me shivers and substantial chills.
It veered off to the east as one great eye
Marked me there in the gloom, a meal to spy!

Cecily

I dreamed a girl from Thessaly
    Came to me one cool dawn,
And loved me there incessantly
    Upon the dewy lawn.

She said her name was Cecily,
    And paler than a swan.
She whispered oh, so pleasantly;
    I sighed and she was gone.

Then I jumped up now presently,
    To seek her far and wide,
Through all the towns in Thessaly,
    Where she might still abide.

In each dream now, respectively,
    On dream winds I would ride,
Yet she was gone so utterly
    Beyond all Time and tide.

I searched for her incessantly,
    And cried and cried and cried
Where was my lovely Cecily?
    And so it was I died.

The Haunted Inn

On nights when the goblins are vying
    With witches above the old kirk,
When the north wind's both moaning and sighing,
    This cold air cuts through like a dirk.
And under each eave and each rafter
    The gray ghosts have fled all too soon,
With the werewolves all following after
    This huge opal moon.

Now past its old gates made of cedar,
    The dark inn stands alone like some ghost.
I watch as its old sign will titter,
    Blown about by cold gales from the coast.
Within its dank rooms, clad in darkness,
    Gray shadows will lengthen and curl,
As the moonlight reveals in its starkness,
    The ghost of a girl.

She's as lovely and bright as the morning,
    With pale shells that are hung from her ears,
With rings and with jewels she's adorning
    Her slim body before dawn appears.
Her beauty could tame a wild lion,
    Or separate tides from the shore,
Or call down the bright stars of Orion
    To land on the moor.

So tall and so like to a goddess,
    And dressed in pale silks as of old,
With a low-cut and most tempting bodice,
    Adorned with thin strands of pure gold.
And over this inn she will hover
    As the night will grow ever so deep,
In search of her fickle lost lover,
    Which makes her now weep.

I have seen her when dark stars have risen,
    Far out of the North and the West,
As the dusk throws open Death's prison,
    To awaken her from a long rest.
I call out to her there and she sees me,
    And she knows it's not me she will seek,
Yet she smiles and she waves but to tease me,
    Though still she is meek.

On nights when the goblins are vying
    With witches above the old kirk,
When the north wind's both moaning and sighing,
    This cold air cuts through like a dirk.
And under each eave and each rafter
    The gray ghosts have fled all too soon,
With the werewolves all following after,
    This huge opal moon.

Stone Pillars

Off to the east by a rill in the valley
    Where the sea wind sunders the fogs of day,
Where the thrush and the lark through old oaks sally,
    A ghost in the ruins bends to pray.
Up now her eyes will turn toward heaven,
    As sings forlornly this gray cold rill,
About her stone pillars that number seven,
    Under the hill.

She's slim and sleek as the willows near her,
    That bend and sway in the soft slow breeze.
She prays alone as the spirits fear her,
    When she comes at dawn through the tall trim trees.
A path winds east to rise up slowly,
    Like the slow small steps of a ladder's rung,
Where this girl died meanly, sadly, lowly,
    On the gibbet hung.

Only the night like a blanket cooling
    This valley and ruin where she bled,
With the moon through the clouds with gray light pooling,
    May conjure such ghosts and wake the dead.
Yet here she kneels in the new born morning.
    So lovely her ghostly and yellow hair,
An ornament for this place adorning
    The day with prayer.

A sigh is heard with the cool breeze moaning,
    Over the stones of this granite pile.
She whispers her prayers on the air intoning;
    Then raises her head to show her smile.
With joy she stands, the earth to embolden,
    Her lungs take in the sweet scent of air,
She throws back her head in a cascade of golden
    Flowing hair.

The Haunted Archipelago

Past islands in a twisting chain
    My ghost ship sails each May,
I seek my tall tanned chatelaine,
    Who went so far away.

Past breakers and the Siren's lure
    I'm stalwart through dismay.
I cast my gaze across each shore
    Where she once went astray.

I tack my ship past headland, reef.
    We met in old Bombay.
I loved her well, though it was brief,
    And then she went away.

And through the nights I chart the stars,
    And weep the livelong day.
I may as well search crimson Mars,
    For she is gone away.

About each cove I search for her,
    And through each sheltered bay,
The sea breeze scented with her myrrh,
    Procured in old Cathay.

I know I'm close, that I will find
    Her soon at work or play.
Her love to mine I'll wed and bind,
    I know I'll find a way!

Then on an island choked with pines,
    I went ashore one day.
At dusk when moonlit silver tines
    Made such an odd display.

I found a pert girl bold as brass,
    A daughter of the Fay.
So supple, slim, sat in the grass,
    Her giant eyes were gray.

"You are a fool for on these coasts,
    There's nothing to survey,
But gauzy, dead, forgotten ghosts,
    Your love's blown far away."

Past islands in a twisting chain
    My ghost ship sails each May,
I seek my tall tanned chatelaine,
    Who went so far away.

When Wizards Meet

I met another man who walked alone
Upon these winding trails deep in the hills.
He told me that he mastered magic skills,
Yet I heard, within his quavering tone,
He only half believed that he had grown
A mage, who conjures imps or quickly kills
His foes, while all the hapless throng so thrills
That scarce they think of him as flesh and bone.

I stared at him long minutes and I sighed.
He reached within his robes to find some prop,
When with a word I made the fellow glide
Far upwards like a child's bright spinning top.
He cursed me, so I turned him to a toad,
And left him there, alone, beside the road.

Lyonnesse

And in my dream I felt her lips caress
My cheek as we stood by the cold seaside.
Enfleshed, she was my slender spirit guide,
For she would show me now lost Lyonnesse.
She took me by the hand. Her blue silk dress
So like the color of the giant tide.
Into the sea, and now the wildest ride,
My will was gone, to hers I'd acquiesce!

I saw the halls were Merlin walked, and kings
Both known and unfamiliar in the deep,
Entombed within the wide concentric rings,
Where princesses and magic Merlin sleep.
Surprised was I to see the tall sea grass
Throng in the courtyards where the stingrays pass.

A Careless Kiss

Where continents have risen, dark seas rolled,
And mighty fleets have come through storm and squall,
Led by some great king, or his seneschal,
To storm some citadel or high stronghold.
I've marked the racing ages as they've scrolled,
From Edo to Pompeii to Senegal,
The vanity of things imperial,
The worthlessness of power and of gold.

And what of me, whose kingdom, like the dust
Is swept away to a far, haunted sea,
And vanished like my unrelenting lust,
My silver, gold, and splintered ivory?
My ghost alone will muse and reminisce,
And all betrayed by one tart's careless kiss.

A Dream of Gold

From dreams I've dredged an ancient mine,
Where some pale sorceress foretold
Such metals I could here refine
The ultimate in precious gold.

I took the heavy blackened ore
To ships and watched their sails unfurled
Then off to some enchanted shore,
Where strange seas lapped a haunted world.

Off loaded all my precious hoard,
And did the things that I was told.
Left all my ships securely moored,
Then set off inland with this gold.

A week through jungles plagued with snakes,
Our guides would caution, curse and scold,
We skirted large and poisoned lakes,
And closer did we guard our gold.

Then two weeks through a desert vast,
So vast that it was hard to hold
Our sanity which ebbed too fast,
As we held close our wondrous gold.

Then one by one our guides all died,
I cursed that sorceress, her kind,
I knew our bones would long abide
With eyeless skulls grown pale and blind.

From dreams I've dredged an ancient mine,
Where some pale sorceress foretold
Such metals I could here refine
The ultimate in precious gold.

A Centauress

At dusk I bathe within the cooling pool.
My dainty hooves step softly in the silt,
And as the curlews cry, my head atilt,
I wash my raven hair and softly mewl.
My grief is for that brave, strong, human boy,
And as I wash my breasts and gleaming flanks
I think of him who loved me on these banks,
He was my one true love, my life, my joy!

He told me I was lovely. I was sleek.
He thought me a proud goddess in disguise.
He brushed my flanks until my knees grew weak,
He held me softly, gently kissed my eyes.
Then he left, the great art of war to learn,
And so I weep for he did not return.

On Wings of Steel

I've seen the sandy slurry slide
Across the lava-leveled plain.
The Earth was new and life untried
Until a tiny protein chain
Was formed so life might there abide.

Where late the magma rolled to hills
Beyond the headland and the tor,
There molten rock left thrifty rills,
A winding basalt corridor,
Where lethal gas a vent distills.

And I soared low with wings of steel
To watch the liquid stone aboil,
While echoing harsh peal on peal
I watched the nickel-iron broil
Where long rift valleys ooze and reel.

And then the Earth, like ice, went cold,
Strong winds now hammered all the crust,
Here Time endeavored to unfold
Below stark peaks as red as rust
Upon long plains of glowing gold.

The Dawn

I ride my barque across the skies.
Below, dark jungles, the baboon
With mouth agape and rolling eyes,
Peals long in terror at the Moon.

I look down at the rampant lion
Who roars in fear, the dead to wake.
Starlight from a bright Orion
Fills all the still and polished lake.

In fear the coiling cobra hides,
His chambered heart now stony cold,
While on the starry ether rides
My barque that's loaded down with gold.

My oarsmen pull across the vast,
Their lips are dumb, their faces wan.
I stand before my soaring mast,
Go down to glory in the dawn.

The Return

Shrill trumpets echoed down the wide-paved mall.
The strumpets, squealing, lined the balconies.
Acacias near the fane swayed in the breeze,
The way was carpeted down each broad hall.

The brooding clouds, unmoving, seemed a pall.
In blue-green pools girls waded to their knees,
Their lords, half drunk, mumbled vague blasphemies;
Horns echoing, echoing overall.

"He has returned, returned!" The cry went up.
The palace guard raised high their two-edged swords.
Each seneschal poured wine into his cup,
Then called in triumph to their torpid lords:
"He has come back, yes, come back from the grave!"
But no soul stirred along that stony pave.

Angels of Ice

Dreams of the tundra lull me alone;
The West Wind sighs with a slow soothing moan;
Sly shadows gather
With potent allure,
Mix with the lather
Of this foaming shore.

Like angels of ice the snow's in accord
With Dreamland's powers sharp as a sword.
While under the awning
Of this ebon scene,
Daylight is dawning
In winter's demesne.

Come give me a cup of the rarest rare wine!
Come give me a kiss and show me a sign,
That in this gloaming
Here under red Mars,
I'll continue my roaming
Far out in the stars.

Cockaigne

The storm winds battered from the south.
The lighthouse light grew weak and dim.
The headland like a corpse's limb
Reached toward the roiling river's mouth.

Tan Sirens on the shore would loll,
Oblivious to cold and storm.
Their magic blood to keep them warm,
They wear the darkness like a shawl.

High in her turret old, arcane,
Yet lovely as a nubile teen,
Pale sorceress with eyes of green
Looks out this night upon Cockaigne.

The city's domes and spires rise.
Svelte sorceress, she broods alone
Within her chamber walled with stone;
Cockaigne's reflected in her eyes.

Her nails are long and polished red;
Her fingers thrum the table's teak.
She holds a mirror there to seek
The beauty of her pretty head.

She smiles as ebon curls uncoil,
Fall free and gently to her cheeks,
Like Aphrodite of the Greeks.
Her skin aglow with precious oil.

The storm begins to rage and roar,
While she, half hearing, breathes a sigh;
One crystal tear from one green eye,
Flows like the tide on some lost shore.

She turns her ermine collar up
Against the night, against the cold;
Her fingers clutch the stem of gold
Upon her tall and wine-filled cup.

In youth she sought love to obtain,
Though now her wine tastes like the dust.
She bartered love for heady lust
Here on the shores of lost Cockaigne.

The Pale Château

I saw the pillars palely glow
With moonlight through the twisted pine.
I watched ten raptors land and crow
All drunk with blood and spilt Bordeaux,
Their eyes aglow with strange starshine.

Above this dream, a dark tableau,
I sensed a presence so malign
From valley to the high plateau,
A nightmare realm so full of woe
That might existence redefine.

Let someone now a boon bestow
Upon this land where grows that vine
Whose grapes of wrath still stretch below
The hoarfrost and push through the snow
To yet distil a deadly wine.

There are no boons to give or know;
No fruits to eat but only swine
Who wander ever to and fro
About the pillared pale château,
Ah, bitter as the salty brine!

Nymphs

On the frigid midnight air
Near the fallen turret's spire,
Phantoms took me unaware
Round the gates of ancient Tyre.

Near the fallen turret's spire
Smoky fragments of a dream
Round the gates of ancient Tyre
Drift along a silent stream.

Smoky fragments of a dream
Thrill me to a quick suspire,
Drift along a silent stream,
Burn me with an ice-cold fire.

Thrill me to a quick suspire
Did the vision in the glade.
Burn me with an ice-cold fire,
Woo me with a serenade!

Did the vision in the glade
Come from valleys of the Fay?
Woo me with a serenade,
Here to love and ever stay.

Come from valleys of the Fay
Sweet nymphs of my own desire,
Here to love and ever stay,
Play your pipes and silver lyre!

Sweet nymphs of my own desire
Lie here in the tall oak's shade,
Play your pipes and silver lyre,
Stay here in this rushy glade.

Lie here in the tall oak's shade,
Hear the gently bleating sheep,
Stay here in this rushy glade,
Till your eyes are filled with sleep!

Hear the gently bleating sheep
Play until the sunset dies,
Till your eyes are filled with sleep,
Till your dreams are filled with sighs.

Play until the sunset dies
Lyre and your reed pipes then
Till your dreams are filled with sighs
Mingled with the thrush and wren.

Lyre and your reed pipes then
Carry tunes upon the breeze,
Mingled with the thrush and wren
Singing there among the trees.

Carry tunes upon the breeze
Sweet nymphs of a sweet allure,
Singing there among the trees
Sirens from a distant shore!

Sweet nymphs of a sweet allure,
Love me with an earnest will!
Sirens from a distant shore,
Love me till the world is still!

Love me with an earnest will
While I kiss your hands and face;
Love me till the world is still,
Jeweled in jade and tatted lace.

While I kiss your hands and face,
Long and lavish crimson hair,
Jeweled in jade and tatted lace,
Drown me, make me gulp for air!

Long and lavish crimson hair
Like a never-lapsing tide,
Drown me, make me gulp for air,
Never will this sea subside!

Like a never lapsing tide
Never will my praises fail;
Never will this sea subside,
Always will my love prevail.

Never will my praises fail
Till the seas are deserts dry;
Always will my love prevail,
Till the stars flee from the sky.

Till the seas are deserts dry,
All's forgotten from the prime,
Till the stars flee from the sky,
Love will last outside of Time!

I Circle Methane Seas

I mark two moons of Saturn, black and teal,
Collide at speed with meteors and more.
I watch it all from this fantastic shore,
From realms outré, obtuse, sidereal.
Above me here the heaven's titan pall,
So like a vaulted tomb where comets soar,
And with these worlds I know an odd rapport,
And think myself some dream-bound sentinel.

I circle methane seas whose mighty tides
All pulled by moons beneath this sable void,
While through the dust it's I who veers and rides
The icy dawns through worlds long since destroyed.
I'm ripped away by forces scarcely known,
To drift away a cold and lifeless stone.

The Lover's Curse

A dream whose dimensions defy human thought
    I dream in the dark and the cold.
It's the curse of a lover whose love I once bought

And I found myself there in an awful web caught,
    For only dark love is so sold.

Down alleyways there in some city unguessed,
    I moil and I look for her there.
As she and her sisters, half pale, half undressed,
Here hawk all their wares without the least zest,
    In cloying and perfumed cool air.

I ask Esmeralda who proffers me more
    Than is right or ever is meet,
If she is the vixen, the dark paramour,
Who calls me each night to this witch-haunted shore,
    That my sorrow might be most complete.

Her huge eyes are dead, and she stares and she stares,
    And nothing in her may I stir.
I can see that she's caught in such abstruse despairs
That she thinks not of me, and for no man she cares.
    I know my curse comes not from her.

Then I meet old Eileen and then young Isabel,
    And my face to them seems most unknown.
And countless old lovers I meet cannot tell
That it's I who's been cursed by some harlot's harsh spell,
    And I feel so intensely alone.

The night and the dark, that iniquitous curse,
    These press me like slabs of huge stone.
And there on that street is a horse-pulled black hearse,

Each horse is a skeleton making it worse,
    And the coachman is wan as pale bone!

I hear a soft voice as it speaks in the night:
    "You were a devil to me!"
I know it is Anna and recall her dark plight,
And I know I was cruel and hurt her for spite,
    Her ghost I can now never flee.

A dream whose dimensions defy human thought
    I dream in the dark and the cold.
It's the curse of a lover whose love I once bought
And I found myself there in an awful web caught,
    For only dark love is so sold.

I Wander

I wandered in the meadow,
I wandered in the lea,
A light and airy feather,
I blushed to see the sea.
And round the granite towers
That rise up to the clouds,
I moved through yellow flowers
Where shadows fell like shrouds.
Above these sandy beaches
I called out to the tides;
My lonely echo reaches
A thousand widowed brides.

I wandered in the meadow
Until the twilight fell
Upon this coast and headland,
Down to the haunted dell.
This night became a dead land,
Yet why, I cannot tell. . . .

The Satrap

The satrap bade his wizards counsel him,
With means to bring a coy girl to his thought.
They warned that magics such as these were fraught
With consequences often random, grim.
He paid no heed but wanted that girl slim
And lovely whom he found could not be bought,
Would now be snared with magic and be caught.
He would possess her heart, each lovely limb.

And so it was his wizards worked a spell,
She loved him then and cried "Yes, you're the one!"
He had six others, now a seventh wife,
And yet, in time, as many could foretell,
She threw off the skein of automaton
And pierced his heart with his own royal knife.

My Dreams Take Me

My dreams take me to eerie lands remote,
To châteaux walled with hand-hewn granite stone,

And often I will wander there alone
To watch the scudding cloudheads as they float.
One eve I came upon a castle's moat,
And it was dry; its drawbridge had been thrown
Wide open, so I crossed it on my own,
Then felt an icy tingle in my throat.

A girl came out, so tall and lovely there,
Her every curve a stirring temptress shape,
With flowing waist-length scarlet-scented hair.
Bewitched I stood agog, my jaw agape.
Her thrilling voice spoke: "What is it you seek?"
I stood so ramrod straight, yet could not speak.

The Ghost Army

I watched that old, slain army there decamp;
They struck their ashen tents without a sound.
I saw them quickly leap and run and bound,
Stand in formation at the end of camp.
Then they moved out to silent shouts. The tramp
Of ghostly boots by rising winds were drowned.
I marked the ghost of one stray eager hound
Mind well a sergeant with his lifted lamp.

They moved away most briskly, with the pall
Of sable starry heavens overhead;
I noted well the fields of grain that sprawl
Beyond their camp site, now where marched the dead.

And underneath the moon's pale watchful eye,
I thought I heard that army breathe a sigh.

Ride the Night Wind

Over deserts, over plains,
    Over rivers, over moors,
She waits past the low moraines,
    Hard by snowy, haunted tors.

On the storm wind, on the waves,
    Over grassland, over seas,
Over grain fields, over graves,
    She waits in the fallow leas.

Ride the thermals, ride the storm,
    Ride the night wind on the air,
Ring the bell and staunch all harm,
    Save me from a black despair.

Now kiss her hands and kiss her eyes,
    Kiss her ectoplasmic lips;
On these thermals she will rise,
    Gold chains on her pallid hips.

Ears bejeweled and eyes that shine,
    Painted cheeks and painted mouth,
Lips like unto agèd wine
    Pressed from vineyards in the south.

Legs with coiling snakes tattooed
     Crush me in your adder's grasp!
Save me from my solitude,
     My poor heart now tightly clasp!

Over deserts, over plains,
     Over rivers, over moors,
She waits past the low moraines,
     Hard by snowy, haunted tors.

Dispatched

The wizard long pursued me through the sand,
Of burning haunted deserts lone and vast.
Yet I eluded him, back through the Past,
With such dark talismans that I command.
I grew weary and so I took a stand
Before huge hulking idols that were cast
In bronze, whose ugliness was unsurpassed,
With Cyclops eyes, their metal deeply tanned.

Then out of spooling dust storms came the mage.
His frame so skeletal and slightly bent;
His eyes burned redly with titanic rage.
His words a hail of arrows quickly sent
That would dispatch me there before the dusk,
Where even now I lie, a withered husk.

Out of the Mountain Pool

She pulled me deep into her mountain pool,
Down, down into a realm unknown to man,
And I met all her kind, her fairy clan,
Yet she was loveliest, a priceless jewel.
Although her father wed us, she was cruel
To keep me there for such a long, long span;
So when the chance arose I left and ran,
So far away to glens remote and cool.

I hid within a cleft within the stone
And prayed that from her wrath I might be spared;
I lived for years on berries, there alone.
One night I saw her, tall and golden-haired,
And standing by the entrance to my cave,
Which, sadly, has become my makeshift grave.

The Call of Orion

Orion calls me. I will go
Beyond the high horizon's limn,
Where star streams filled with beauty flow
And avid avatars yet swim.

Brown nebula, they eye me there,
Above this incandescent sea.
I long to drown in Psyche's hair
And lose myself so utterly!

Sweet Sirens proffer drinks to me,
Each offering to make me stay.
I'm filled with pride stupendously,
And yet I would be far away.

Orion calls me. I will go
Beyond the high horizon's limn,
Where star streams filled with beauty flow
And avid avatars yet swim.

Like a Stone

I climb this cliff-face high, in bitter cold;
These soaring Pteranodons now eye me there,
Their necks and bodies leathery and spare,
And every minute they become more bold.
Yet still I climb, as I have done of old;
A fool, I've hung within this cooling air,
Till now I verge upon a black despair;
My strength is gone, my fingers lose their hold.

I plummet seaward where the moon's pale kiss
Is set upon these waves within the brine.
Now soon I'll drown within that cold abyss,
No more to see the moon or gold sun shine,
And like a stone it there will bury me
Some time lost Icarus drowned in the sea.

Girl from Altair

I trek through dreams entire
    To seek for lovers there;
Until the stars expire,
    I seek them everywhere.

My belly full of fire,
    I breathe a rarer air
And court death with desire
    In magic perfumed hair.

Such Sirens here suspire
    Beneath this moonlit glare,
Their love both hot and dire,
    Some dusky, others fair.

Some see me as their squire,
    Their gaze but few can bear;
Such beauty all admire,
    So sly and sleek and spare.

Come soon, for I require
    Your love brought from Altair,
For I both shake, perspire;
    Your sigh like some sweet prayer.

I trek through dreams entire
    To seek for lovers there;

Until the stars expire,
    I seek them everywhere.

Like Solomon

Upon an eminence windswept and cold
I stood alone to watch Orion climb,
And spoke a spell obtuse, arcane, sublime;
Then round that height strange spirits there patrolled.
I conjured there a lover, sleek and bold;
I called her out of Space and out of Time,
A wife of Solomon, back in the prime,
With eyes like roiling seas, whose hair was gold.

She wore huge opals, bangles on each wrist,
And little else but her bewitching smile.
I could not speak before I had been kissed!
She chained me with her monumental guile.
Deep in my heart some magic then would stir,
Like Solomon, I fell a slave to her.

Ghost of the Fen

Dusk is drear as the wan moon rises,
    Wan and hornèd, drear and pale.
There on the marge my lover rises,
    Her hair like a ghostly billowed sail.

All night long by this cold fen wooing,
Ever her love I am pursuing,
Cold her kisses, yet soft her cooing,
    A wispy ghost both strong, yet frail.

Here in the winter darkness strolling,
    Under a moon of skulls we go,
While yonder is that cold sea rolling,
    Its whitecaps breaking wan as snow.
Out from the fen we march alluring
    Ghost and ghouls their rest procuring;
They see us now, mad ghouls go roaring,
    There as the ceaseless cold winds blow.

Only gray moonlight is her cover,
    Here as we walk in snow like sand;
A pledge of love to my pale lover,
    I bend to kiss her ice cold hand.
Then in the shadows whispers hearing,
There at the edge of simple fearing,
Words of the dead now floating, nearing,
    Say that such love is evil, banned!

And then to me my lover turning,
    A whispered word that she will leave,
All of my heart within me burning,
    I pull on her frail and wan white sleeve.
Then she whispered me, "It's forbidden,
None may rise from the dead unbidden,
For such dark lore must needs be hidden,
    Though my cold heart for thee doth grieve!"

Dusk is drear as the wan moon rises,
    Wan and hornèd, drear and pale.
There on the marge my lover rises,
    Her hair like a ghostly billowed sail.
All night long by this cold fen wooing,
Ever her love I am pursuing,
Cold her kisses, yet soft her cooing,
    A wispy ghost both strong, yet frail.

Haunted

I found the ancient chalice in the soil
Where once a temple spanned this sandy vale.
My mind's eye saw a girl so slim and pale,
Her hair was silky black with perfumed oil.
The noonday sun was hot, and in this broil
Of summer heat she held that silver grail.
I saw her drain it through her sheer white veil
This same old chalice that my hands despoil.

Down dizzy centuries remote from us,
Alone, she stalks the vanished temple still.
And all for love, ah, it is ever thus!
I see her move with an uncommon skill,
She but a slave, her love a shiftless thief.
Oh, how she moves me with a nameless grief!

The Crystal Flame

Among the Stars

Among some stars remote, gargantuan,
Is sung from one stupendous, mighty throat,
Down the lost years, this long-ago sung note.
A bow across some titan violin
Produces music where the red dwarves spin
In galaxies impossibly remote.
Where long-dead drifting worlds forever float
As dense as ancient lead, as light as tin.

And in one constellation there depends
An opal moon gigantic as our sun,
So huge the very space and light it bends.
It's here I'll swim until all time is done
To watch as each soul plummets or ascends
And then watch all fold to oblivion.

In Nan Modal

Before a line of weaving slaves, your fan
Hid your shy face before the moiling throng,
Though they were fain to carry you along,
Upon your sleek and silver-chased divan.
A sun roof of fine-woven blue rattan
Protected you from rays both hot and strong;
All worshipped you to clamors from a gong,
Both slaves and royalty down to a man.

* * *

Along the green lagoon sit huge canoes.
They've come to Nan Modal from distant seas:
Ten thousand soldiers on the banks, in queues,
Line up to pledge their love and fealties.
They put you down, you stand, and your tattoos
Reveal your many potent sorceries.

The Dream Rider

Across the roads of destiny,
Under the stars aglint,
I've come this night across the sea,
My heart as hard as flint.

Above the stars that reel and glow,
I hear the pounding sea,
The distant tor is wan with snow
To light my destiny!

Along the trail, the mournful wail,
A werewolf in the glen.
His midnight song's of no avail
Deep huddled in his den.

I take the turn down that ravine
Hard by the haunted yew;
Here I recall the Shadow Queen,
With cunning eyes of blue!

Behind the agèd oak-hewn door,
Within the crumbled wall,
I once met with my paramour,
Across a flagstone mall.

I ride, I ride and ride on down
Under some lunar spell,
There a girl in a pale green gown
Floats from a haunted well.

Over the valleys to the cliffs,
There in the cold night air,
Gray ghosts sail by in spectral skiffs,
Led by a wan corsair.

From out the stars a solar chime
Arrives with each moonbeam,
And I have lost my race with Time,
So now I ride in dream.

Ghost Kings of Mu

They say its shores held golden sand.
Its rivers were both long and wide,
Its palaces framed all that land
And filled its royalty with pride.
Upon its saffron seas would glide
Tall ships with sails in pale pastels

That came in with the foaming tide
To trumpets and the clang of bells.

In dreams I see its towers sway
Atop the chalk cliff palisade,
While far below the spume and spray
Dance in a salty spry charade,
Anoint each titan colonnade.
And then I watch long shadows fall
On aisles of palaces arrayed
With porticoes across the mall.

Mile-high redoubts, each sloping wall
Of finely quarried, polished stone,
The frightened fishes now appall.
All now are gone, long overthrown,
And all their grandeur long since flown
Though once they reigned a thousand years;
But now their salty sunken throne
Is watered with a sea of tears.

That continent has long since died,
To live in dreams, the sea's blue brine,
Where that colossus took in stride
Its sovereignty and did assign
Itself a place with the divine.
Their mighty kings sought to compel
The very seas with spells malign,
Threw down their gods to deepest hell.

Alas, for that poor continent!
No more its fleets will span the seas.
Its ghosts are still impenitent
And haunt dreams like a dark disease
To fill our thoughts with fantasies.
Still on the demon wind they ride,
And whisper on the midnight breeze,
They know not yet that Mu has died.

Atlantis

Cities of gold and ivory antique,
Your promenades of polished stone still yawn
Across those dreams where crystal visions spawn
Chryselephantine worlds outré, unique.
Each temple dome rose like some mountain peak.
Those toppled topless towers long since gone
Know nevermore the flame-tongued crimson dawn,
Though still lives on your magical mystique.

When moon and stars at solstice now align,
I hear your old and cryptic, mantic name
Whispered among the low hills where the pine
And oaks recall your spires' ancient fame;
Then for a moment in the dark I see
Atlantis rise again in majesty!

Strange Harbor

I led a fleet of galleys toward the dawn.
The morning stars, like beacons deftly hung,
Fled like the awful misbegotten spawn
That gods from distant worlds had long since flung.
My fleet by some celestial magics drawn
Was pulled by unseen string by magi strung,
String spooled by that great desert god, Amon,
In seasons when his harvest hymns were sung.

At length we harbored on a distant shore
Where mighty peaks tore at the burning sky,
And there were silver Sirens by the score
Who all were lean and tall and sleek and sly.
I came ashore and crossed an icy stream
And entered then an unknown realm of dream.

The Nymph's Prayer

Find me a canyon,
Here in my dream,
Where an old banyan
Stands by a stream.

Find me in twilight
Under red Mars,
There in a highlight,
A place that is ours.

Dream me a lover
Soft and remote,
One like no other
With gems on his throat.

Take me to castles
Out on the grange;
Banish the vassals
Loves rearrange!

Lave me with lotions,
Spicy and pure
There by strange oceans,
There on the shore.

Clothe me in dresses
Pale as is milk;
Comb out my tresses
Smooth as is silk.

Meet me in winter
Under this oak;
Moonlight will splinter
To silver my cloak.

Drink me like water
From Neptune's sea.
I am his daughter,
Drink all of me!

Clothe me in fashions
Cool and outré,
Garner my passions,
Then make me stay!

Gather the mountains,
Roll up the moor,
Empty the fountains,
There on the shore!

Call up the ages,
Bar all the tombs,
My love ever rages
Banishing glooms!

Bring back all magic
From years in the Past;
Know it was tragic,
Both tragic and vast!

Bind me in wire
Of finest spun gold,
Come quench my fire
And warm me when cold.

Play on this harp please
Hard by my door;
Banish these harpies
From headland and moor!

Call up the West Wind,
Ravish my hair;
It is the best wind,
Briny sea air!

Teams of tall camels
Loaded and tan,
Hot sand each trammels
My caravan!

Load them with silver
By soldiers patrolled,
Then fill up your quiver
With arrows of gold!

Call down the planets
So far above;
Fracture the granites
And love me, my love!

Grasp me and crush me
In arms of steel;
Kiss me and hush me,
Hear my appeal!

Love me forever
Her on this bay,
Or be then clever
And love for a day!

The Temptress

I dreamed that on a throne of ebony
    A queen to see,
Her regal, scented hair so dark and long,
    Her eyes like dawn.

Her huge and gorgeous eyes were brimming jewels,
    Sweet drowning pools,
Fine and most splendid torques by goldsmiths rolled,
    Her neck wears gold.

Gold chatelaines upon her curving hips,
    Her pouting lips
With henna painted and her cheekbones high
    That make men sigh.

Her legs are long, with toe rings on her toes,
    Bathed in aloes;
Her goddess body scented like the rose,
    Sweet love bestows.

Her skirt of purple silk falls to her thighs;
    She stands, all rise.
With outstretched arms she yawns, and suitors sigh,
    For her they'd die.

A sorceress within her citadel,
    And I can tell,
Her huge eyes brim with love eternally,
    Yet not for me!

A Traveler through Time

In dreams above the walls of Troy
I am a magic snow-white gull,
And then the image I destroy
To soar above old Istanbul.

Against the walls of far Cathay
I heard the sounding clarions,
While on the plains there far away
Huge armies of barbarians.

And then my magic wings would soar
And I would call on Hindustan,
To lost and mythic Rajapore,
On roads where tramped the caravan.

Then Africa became my guide;
At sunset I would make landfall.
Then through the upper air I'd glide
And circle humid Senegal.

To northward I would ride the wind,
Then back in Time to the Levant,
And as the cooling air there thinned
I'd listen to the old monks chant.

To some far future yet unknown
Above a city with no name,
I soared above its black, charred stone,
A holocaust consumed by flame.

Strange Stars

I dreamed of lawns before a monument,
A titan statue that was once patrolled
By hand-picked men who were controlled
By Amazons who ruled that continent.
At night within that inky firmament
Strange stars would swirl as high-priests there cajoled
That granite god whose chest was burnished gold,
To hide an evil heart of vast extent.

I marveled at that strange colossus there—
His spiky head, his granite chiseled toes.
They said he came from out the haunted lake;
I cringed then as he stirred within his chair.
Stone muscles flexed as from that throne he rose,
And as he walked that continent would shake.

In Isfahan

In Isfahan by midnight streams,
We stopped our winding caravan,
And when the stars rose dreamed our dreams
    In Isfahan.

Here through rose gardens swiftly ran
Pale nymphs whose wild romantic schemes
Were part of some enchanted plan.
There in those dreams the pale moonbeams

Fell lightly on the haunts of man
And bathed us all in silver creams
    In Isfahan.

Ganymede

On Ganymede tall women play
When all the summer tides recede,
Down in a warm secluded bay
    On Ganymede.

They dream of love, their only need,
And in the cooling evening pray
Among the marshy spider weed.

I, too, have dreamt of love all day,
Yet find no help, none intercede
To take me there, so far away,
    On Ganymede.

Ulysses

Lashed to the mast I watch each tangled line;
I hear the Sirens singing from the gloom.
My nerves are taut, I nearly taste perfume
Upon a salty breeze that's near divine.
I curse my crew and bid them cut the twine
That holds me vise-like in this hempen womb.

My hair and beard are white with icy spume;
This cloying lust seems like to crush my spine!

I see them on their rocks so lean and pure,
With flesh as pale as sea foam in the sun.
I am enthralled, but know that fatal shore,
That all their love is but oblivion.
The danger gone, we turn the ship alee,
And I am lost and lonely on the sea.

Intruder

She came across some misty borderland
And said that gender was a thing unknown.
They all ate manna from the warm wind blown
That fell on valleys, hills, down to the strand.
She smiled and took me shyly by the hand,
Though as we walked I found that I was prone
To leave this child, a woman scarcely grown;
I felt her presence we could not withstand.

For poverty would end and war would cease,
And all our arms and swords would turn to ploughs.
I'd watch the state all prisoners release,
Men and women exchange true wedding vows.
Such awful things now swirled inside my head.
I left her in the tall grass cold and dead.

Castles in the Air

I dream of Sirens sleek and pale
And floating castles in the air.
I hear my lover's frantic wail,
I dream of Sirens sleek and pale,
And seek her out, and will not fail
For when I hear my lover's hail
I dream of Sirens sleek and pale
And floating castles in the air.

Only an Evil Wind Went Roaring

I dream of her there a pale flower
    Here under the shade of this oak;
In its shadow we spend an hour,
    With wan moonlight she wears as a cloak.
Here all of my hurt she will sever,
Her ardor will last here forever,
A bewitching girl who's twice clever
    To vanish away like blown smoke.

I dream once again, count the hours,
    When strange dawns with gray ghosts arise.
She comes as I learn all her powers,
    Sunk deep in her violet eyes!
I lay in her arms there at leisure,
Such bliss as I know none may measure;

Were paradise such avid pleasure
    I'd die to soar into these skies!

One dusk all my dreams went there soaring
    Until there was nothing left there.
With most savage ill winds blasting, roaring,
    And laughter that hung in the air.
My soul sank despairing, so lowly,
No love for me brightly, or holy;
She was gone, the one I loved solely,
    Left only the scent of her hair.

Spirit Cave

These lonely lovers mouth mute madrigals
As balmy breezes from the cave's mouth lave
The ancient stone of this cold, haunted cave,
And cloak the place in sad and dreary palls.
Somnambulant in dreams I've heard those calls,
And like some long-oppressed and frightened slave
Call to some necromantic antique grave
And blindly grope along the dark cave's walls.

Down that dark valley's brooding titan trees,
Near that cave's mouth, is just the hint of myrrh
Of one whose beauty plotted treacheries
Nearby this twisted, giant conifer.
Now I awake to walls of amethyst:
Mine ancient love, she comes once more to tryst!

Vengeful Vipers Vex All This

Vengeful vipers vex all this vaunted vale
Where wicked wyverns weave wan witches' spells;
Fantastic famished females flee these fells,
While I am left here harried and half hale.
A panoply of playful harlots pale
Sing songs, each of their surly charms here sells.
Their trailing tresses tease, each tartly tells
They mourn to make the most of each mad male!

I run among the harlots, racing round,
Yet cannot cull or kill my lucid lust!
I bow, I cannot breath, I dip, I drown!
I'm ravenous and wretched, thick with rust!
I'm doomed to dark delights and sanguine sighs,
Yet undeterred I dutifully die!

A Vision

Upon the headland hard alee,
Beyond the playing pod of whales,
I saw them gleam like ivory,
Tall ships with square-rigged mighty sails.

For surely this was sorcery?
The far horizon shone like cream;
A thousand ships upon that sea
Were conjured from some amber dream.

I heard the soaring linnets call,
Then echo back from that far coast.
I watched the sea swells rise and fall
And spume spray like an eerie ghost.

Up, up from all that shooting brine
I thought I saw a caliph's tent.
He staggered as though drunk with wine,
Distilled from vineyards near Tashkent.

Upon the headland hard alee,
Beyond the playing pod of whales
I saw them gleam like ivory,
Tall ships with square-rigged mighty sails.

The Fatal Shore

I long to see you once again
Beyond these deserts dry and drear,
And past the witch-cursed, stagnant fen.
I long to see you once again
Out on that island high and clear.

It's past the reef enshrouded shore;
It has been now near one long year
Since black death took you there before,
To that lost island's high clear shore,
Yet I will go despite my fear.

I cross those deserts dry and drear,
Then through that snake-infested fen.
You were so precious and so dear!
I cross those deserts dry and drear,
And I would cross them yet again!

I wade that deep unfathomed fen
And count sad spirits by the score.
I'm blessed more so than other men—
I've come out safely from the fen!
Your memory's a potent lure.

Now on that shore, incessantly,
I call your name once and again.
I mark that island in the sea;
That's why I cry incessantly:
I know none there return again.

Ur

They whisper as they shift these ancient dunes.
I wander here at dusk as once before
I climbed the high-stepped ziggurat of Ur,
Beneath those sleek and slender sickle moons.
And once again that opal orb festoons
These starry heavens far from any shore,
As I am left to seek my paramour
And whisper on the air those arcane runes.

* * *

Her scent is yet so sensual and fresh,
Though forty centuries ago she sighed
At my kisses and those of Gilgamesh,
Before my princess one dark night she died.
Though I yet seek her in this famished land,
My magic's fled, I've none left to command.

Cold Is the River

Cold is the night, cold is this river
    Under this gray-eyed massive moon;
Songs on this breeze make the reeds shiver,
    Words of an old and magic rune.
Into the darkness fast and blurring,
There by the river where it's stirring,
Where councils of ghosts group, conferring,
    There to a reed flute's elfin tune.

Here with the leaden skies as awning,
    Pale nymphs wander now to and fro,
Braiding their hair until the dawning,
    Then go where the dark fauns make them go.
Under these clouds the rain is coming
Where an elf girl her lute is strumming.
She hears the thunder loudly drumming,
    That echoes from the far plateau.

Quickly that elf girl's drenched with showers;
    Little it is in her bright eyes.
She loves both storms and thirsty flowers,
    Nature's her lover, her one prize.
Under the oaks she flees for cover,
There where the pale ghosts brood and hover,
She wrestles with her ardent lover,
    Until the sanguine sun should rise.

In Castles of Steel

I dream of her nightly in castles of steel
    On a cliff in the mist on the bay.
And there she will tease and accost and reveal,
A secret her red lips both seal and unseal,
    That no man might know in the day.

Now her walls they are strung with banners that fold
    Or unfold at a given command.
They are scenes in pastels that both mythic and bold
Are woven with threads of the finest pure gold,
    From looms of some lost fabled land.

She sways as she walks to the beat of my heart,
    While her flesh is pale as the moon.
I am summoned at dusk through her strong magic art,
Then she swears we are one and we never will part!
    Then chants me a fay subtle rune.

And I drink her sweet love right down to the lees,
    Then I float with her off to the stars.
Her love is a spell that hangs high in the breeze
Of typhoon-driven storms on fantastical seas.
    While her hair is as red as red Mars.

I am spent like the gold in some brothel forgot,
    And I wake and it's always the same:
I'm alone in my room on this moth-eaten cot.
I've lost her again. She's left me to rot,
    And I still haven't learned yet her name!

I dream of her nightly in castles of steel
    On a cliff in the mist on the bay,
And there she will tease and accost and reveal,
A secret her red lips both seal and unseal,
    That no man might know in the day.

Realm of Dreams

I've trod the ancient alleys
    Beyond that haunted stream,
Far past deep shadowed valleys
    Into the realm of dream.
It's there I seek her ever
    Where moon-white orchids grow,
Where marshal spirits clever
    Guard her and her chateau.

Her castle rises over
    Both city and the plain.
My cogent agile lover
    Extends her most harsh reign.
These suitors woo her nightly
    Who come up from the shore,
Past orchids glowing whitely
    Across the fen and moor.

They kneel in humble terror
    Before her granite throne;
She's ruled thus for an era,
    By no man overthrown.
I call her from the valley,
    I hail her from the wall,
Where coward suitors sally
    As I curse them one and all.

Come out to me this hour!
    Thy suitors I will slay!
I'll storm both wall and tower,
    My power I'll display!
Her suitors then ran frightened
    Back to that icy shore;
My muscles all then tightened
    As they raced across the moor.

I smashed my fist the harder
    Against her iron door;
It echoed in the larder
    And down each corridor;

It sounded in her tower
>   Then bounced against her floor
And shook the Grecian bower
>   Of my would-be paramour!

She strode her ramparts wholly
>   In anger and with rage;
Screamed: "Thou art most unholy,
>   Thou witless, puny sage!"
She raised her hand quite sweetly
>   And then she signaled me,
And then most savage, fleetly,
>   I was swept far out to sea!

She smiled at me most cruelly.
>   I fought those chilling swells;
I cursed her loudly, duly,
>   With a plethora of yells!
I struggled with the water,
>   An icy oily brown,
And cursed that bastard's daughter
>   As I began to drown.

I've trod the ancient alleys
>   Beyond that haunted stream,
Far past deep shadowed valleys
>   Into the realm of dream.
It's there I seek her ever
>   Where moon-white orchids grow,
Where marshal spirits clever
>   Guard her and her château.

Argosy of Dreams

Below the twisted, spiraled keep,
The cliff-face fronts an ancient sea.
Behind its high slit windows sleep
The strange dreams of some argosy.

The cliff-face fronts an ancient sea.
Thus by this ocean is it kissed,
The strange dreams of some argosy,
And walled with clouds of silver mist.

Thus by this ocean is it kissed,
Strange places sought eternally,
And walled with clouds of silver mist.
Where combers crash infernally.

Strange places sought eternally,
Drawn like some magnet to spring steel,
Where combers crash infernally
To stamp some giant mantic seal.

Drawn like some magnet to spring steel,
While here each spirit plots and schemes
To stamp some giant mantic seal
Upon this argosy of dreams.

While here each spirit plots and schemes
All the blind, the lame, the halt
Upon this argosy of dreams
Ascend these cliffs of grey basalt.

In dream these spirits call to me,
While in this castle walled with sleep,
The cliff face fronts an ancient sea
Below the twisted, spiraled keep.

Centaur Love

On worlds where the marshes are methane-grown grass,
    Its twin suns align ere the dusk.
These stars in this heaven all others surpass.
I dream of an alien bright-eyed young lass
    As pale as our old moon's wan tusk.

Then out of these mists a pale centauress comes,
    And she's pert and a thoroughbred sure.
She holds a gold lute that she so gently strums,
As she trots to me slowly I hear her sweet hums,
    Like some fool her love I implore!

Now she gazes with eyes as cold as blue seas,
    As her hair falls there in cascade.
Her musk and her scent is now blown on the breeze.
I am thralled with such love and desire to please,
    Such a creature as ever God made!

Her gleaming white flanks most hypnotic and fine,
    I'm a slave to her savage wild eyes.
Her fetlocks are ribboned in long scarlet twine.
I know not her groom, yet I wish she were mine,
    And she charms there the pale butterflies!

Come now, sweet centauress, and let me touch thee,
    Ere I die from this fire within!
A pure pretty girl that all eyes now may see.
Please say that you're lonely, and love only me,
    For certain, I'll vow it's no sin!

On worlds where the marshes are methane-grown grass,
    Its twin suns align ere the dusk,
These stars in this heaven all others surpass,
I dream of an alien bright-eyed young lass
    As pale as our old moon's wan tusk.

Barge

Upon the rising river cool
I ride the barge of great Amon.
The sun sets like a giant jewel;
I wait for dawn.

Then at first light I think I see
The god return, the jewel of dawn
Comes up like some great argosy,
Across the lawn.

In Mendes and Lycopolis,
My barge sails like a silver swan
Past Tava and Cynopolis,
And then is gone.

I see the toppled columns rest
Deep in the sand, while winds have drawn
Dunes where each ibis makes its nest,
Strange pantheon!

Uncounted years upon this stream
I spy no more the temple's lawn,
Now all is ruin, like some dream.
I wait for dawn.

Lost World

I left that dream and ever since
    I have not been the same.
I yearn for ancient continents—
    My heart's a burning flame!

It was a realm where pterosaurs
    Rule all that foreign sky,
While dark-eyed girls bask on their shores,
    All fay and sleek and sly.

It's there where billowed clouds of foam
    Rise from its calm seas vast.
That is the place that is my home,
    So far within the Past!

A stranded pilgrim, here I brood,
    For I am cast adrift
Among a people base and crude,
    This world which is no gift.

I long to see the theropod
   Stalk through tall reeds at dawn,
Where strange wild flowers droop and nod
   Above a sea-green lawn.

I loved to watch the ships that sailed
   To ports now long since gone,
And loved to hear when seamen wailed
   At sight of Megalodon!

Huge conifers grew tall and green
   Against the cliffs at dusk,
While from the sky a light pristine
   Shone from the pale moon's tusk.

Ah, pain so deep I cannot think!
   No words to form my tale.
Into despair I sadly sink
   As I grow thin and pale!

Ah, send me back to that far land
   That smells of primal things!
I see me standing on that strand
   In my rememberings!

Would that the world were different here;
   And yet, it is not so.
I crave that lost world, fine and dear.
   I must not stay, but go!

I left that dream and ever since
    I have not been the same.
I yearn for ancient continents—
    My heart's a burning flame!

The Glen

Here in this necromantic glen
Where seven silver songbirds sing,
I see a golden-breasted wren
Here in this necromantic glen,
And I am taken home again,
Upon each frail and feathered wing
Here in this necromantic glen
Where seven silver songbirds sing.

The Harpy

Deep in a hazy dark far dream
I walked the slate-gray esplanade,
Down to a rushing silver stream,
Before a temple's stone façade.

A harpy made of granite stone
Tilted there in summer's dusk;
A slight breeze seemed to make her moan
Below the sharp moon's sanguine tusk.

Gargoyle

That statue had some inner pull
That to me seemed both magic, odd:
Quite muscular, yet beautiful,
She, half a harpy, half a god.

I stared long at her shadowed eyes;
The gray-blind stone looked slightly flawed,
And then I saw her stone lids rise,
And I gaped there both stunned and awed!

She stretched her arms and moved her hands;
Her slender fingers savage, clawed.
About each leg a silver band
Wound tightly round each thigh most broad.

She shook her head and pretty hair;
Her shoulders, breasts would there maraud,
And lovely scents then filled the air.
It seemed the stars might give her laud!

She stepped from off her pedestal,
Alit upon the gray-slate quad,
And agilely moved with a will
Like some athletic female god.

I trembled with slight fear as she
Brushed past me with her unclothed flesh.
Her tight tanned skin felt warm to me;
She seem like spring, both swift and fresh!

She turned then slightly as to look,
Gave me a gaze of one who's bored,
And then it was her leave she took,
Scarce knowing that she was adored!

Elemental

I washed ashore ten thousand years ago
Upon the Nile's huge delta when it bore
Lush crops and teeming peoples by the score:
This was the sacred Nile's life-giving flow.
I stayed for centuries, saw great Pharaoh
Who first proclaimed himself a god before
His worshippers who chanted in a roar:
I frowned to watch his awful ego grow.

I used my powers with his lovely wife,
A dusky child as pretty as the stars;
I caused the girl one night to plunge a knife
Into his heart when first ascended Mars.
And though quite young she proved herself most sage,
I let her rule benignly for an age.

I Have Danced with Princesses

Upon the wings of dragons I have flown
Above the isles where wanton harpies nest;
I've slept upon a harlot's tattooed breast
And quarried idols from basaltic stone.

I've heard the heads on Easter Island grown
When giant storm-clouds up rose in the West,
And I have danced with princesses who dressed
In nothing but the moonlight when alone.

On hillocks in a valley lost to Time
Wan nymphs will call for me when comes the Spring:
They crown my head with myrtle and with thyme
And dance for me and seat me as their king.
Then in the fall they take me to their stream
And banish me from out that realm of dream.

The Haunted Temple

This temple's portico now fronts this lake,
Its columns totter from long disrepair,
Its roof is gone, thick ivy lends despair
To its cracked marble walls that, weathered, break
In winter, when the icy rains will slake
The thirsty earth and dampen all the air.
At night the moon, like some god's eye, will stare,
And pale ghosts sigh for that sad temple's sake.

A home to foxes and the vagrant wren,
Its confines damp and thick with loamy must
That seeps in from the nearby growing fen:
It worshippers are now but slime and dust;
A lovely ghost here sings a madrigal
Against the day that fane will crash and fall.

The Sorceress at the End of Space-Time

My ghost will mount these gray and distant stars
As I move through the dust-clouds azurine.
The shells of starships builded on red Mars
Drift past me hulking, dead, and half-obscene.
I do not know what quest has thralled my heart,
My heart of hard and burnished, glowing brass,
Nor does this dusty detritus reveal, impart
A clue—I'm blind before a looking-glass!
I circle Vega, yet its heat's grown cold,
And why I move and climb I cannot tell;
The starlight frames me in a wreath of gold,
And yet my dead heart beats, a silent bell.
I think, perhaps I know, on distant shores
Of moons that circle there, relentlessly,
I'll find beyond a field of meteors
A sad and cold and Siren-haunted sea.
For now the crystal star-streams gleam
So far ahead it seems I'll never rise
To those far shores that touch the realm of dream
That hint, but only hint, of Paradise.
I ride a comet's tail of brilliant ice
Past burning pulsars in the furthest void;
An ancient ship, a thing of rare device,
Sails past a red and fractured planetoid;
It hurtles toward the nearby Betelgeuse,
Where dead worlds circle coldly to the West.
I find them empty, dry, of little use,

And leave them to their ancient, interred rest.
And then my comet marks a great gray ship
Wherein a race of beings once surveyed
Far realms unknown, unguessed, while Time would slip
And net them in Death's treacherous cascade.
This ship I enter through its gaping side
And let my giant, sailing comet go;
Now through this long-dead ship I walk and glide,
Its rusted walls half-white as new-made snow,
In twisted heaps their skeletons all tied
To chair and braces like to polished steel.
It's been three million years since they have died;
This scene is outré and is most surreal.
My ghostly finger touches one odd bone,
My faux lungs oddly seem to fill with air;
I hear a soft and gentle, plaintive tone
And see a lovely vision standing there.
The female of the species, tall and lean,
One Cyclops eye within her pretty head,
Her hair like well-combed kelp, a lucid green,
Her soft flesh oddly colored, like to lead.
She sings a soft brief song, so like a call,
That fills me with remorse and half with fear;
My ghost eyes weep before this madrigal.
In icy space I shed an icy tear;
I cannot bear such sorrow from the Past—
It stabs me with a scimitar of pain.
I quit that dead ship, and I quit it fast,
For such I think that God would prompt, ordain.

I soar the zeniths of the spheres once more,

I drop like lightning to the far abyss,

My ghostly ears now filling with a roar,

I feel the heat of starlight's burning kiss.

Imperial my thoughts as I ascend

And mount the highest stars that ever were;

About me Space and Time they tear and bend,

And sleeping gods begin to wake and stir!

I circle valleys round a half-dead star

Upon a world where shadows are the norm,

A place destroyed by unimagined war,

A stark, cold world, where little's left that's warm.

So I descend through valleys where a cave

Whose alabaster walls have led me now,

A broken statue on an antique grave,

The stone's hard face, a grim and beetled brow,

That tells its king, a monster, harshly ruled.

I quivered in the darkness with him there,

And saw his spirit rise! It spooled, unspooled,

Then vanished in that haunted, icy air!

Then by his cold and alabaster tomb I saw,

Above a black and oily-looking pool,

A magic thing, outside of any law,

A round and red, and spinning potent jewel!

I plucked the jewel of Time in my cold hands

And felt myself some captain at the helm,

And then I whispered grave arcane commands,

Then entered into some benighted realm.

The world went cold, yes, colder than my ghost!

I heard a methane ocean roaring there,
I found myself upon a vasty coast,
With terradons high soaring in the air!
And then it was much to my huge surprise,
They eyed me there on that volcanic shore—
Indeed, they fixed me in their giant eyes,
Then swooped down, this intruder to explore!
The first to reach me tore into my arm!
And filled with terror—was I not a ghost?
They could, it seemed, do any spirit harm;
I dropped that magic jewel there on the coast!
I fled across the land to mount the dawn,
I soared high to the upper atmosphere;
In hot pursuit those terradons came on,
Yet I flew high and watched them disappear.
And now into Space-Time of unknown hue
I sojourned in this world most magical;
My nameless quest I once again renew,
Although it seems absurd and tragical.
I passed a moon where crowds thronged near and far,
In sprawling cities teeming on the plain,
And all lit warmly by its titan star,
With oceans pale as ever was champagne.
Their temples thronged the hills and thronged the sea,
Their massive domes all painted gold and cream,
And each façade of purple porphyry,
Each temple there a doorway to a dream!
My ghost will mount these gray and distant stars
Once more though dust clouds white and azurine.

The shells of starships builded on red Mars
Drift past me hulking, dead, and half-obscene.
I do not know what quest still thralled my heart,
My heart of hard and burnished, glowing brass,
Though in this place, once more I start
My quest, and watch the sailing planets pass.
I turned to hear odd whale-song lingering
And groaning at the edge of Time itself,
As I recalled with just the slightest sting
Their bones that made for frivolous wan pelf.
I thrilled to see their ghosts, so broad in beam,
And gaped to see each huge cetacean head;
They toured the stars in some forgotten dream,
These monsters of the sad and regal dead.
Below me on a sandy arid plain
I felt a tugging at my icy heart;
So far below me where great rivers drain,
A wealth of wizards hawking at some mart.
Adown the icy clouds I plummet there,
This planet lit by one stupendous star;
I land upon that plain in hot dry air,
To move among the booths in that bazaar.
I wander through that throng now all unseen
And note the wizards' pyramidal hats;
Their robes are cinnabar and yellow-green,
While some sit on most finely woven mats.
Then one old wizened seer looks in my eye:
"Come hither, ghost, look here now and take note,
For I have plucked such magic from the sky,

Which hangs upon this chain about my throat."
I gazed into his moonstone, could not move;
I felt a most centripetal strong pull,
And like or not, his magics I would prove,
Sucked into some pale eyeless grinning skull!
I found myself in snowfields on some isle,
Beyond all Space and Time, a wretched soul,
Yet there before me, so lovely in her guile,
A sorceress stood tall and sleek and whole!
She wore a coat of wool and ermine made,
Her beauty seemed a shocking pure surprise,
I noted well blue gems in each long braid
And, too, I saw the power in her eyes!
"Take me, now!" I shouted to the Lord,
"For I can no more think, nor yet go on,
Slay me with your sharp and righteous sword,
That I may enter then oblivion!"
Yet death came not, and this I haply tell,
That she was wed and bonded then to me,
And for eternity we two may dwell
Upon this isle, hard by this unknown sea.

The Seneschal

Under the idol's head I hear,
When silent shadows stretch and strain,
The iron chain about his ear
That rusts with years of icy rain.

And as he tilts to westward there
Under an evil wayward star,
The moss grows thick about his hair,
His face grown dark as with hot tar.
I come each dusk, alone recall,
Below his massive granite head,
That I was once his seneschal,
Though I am centuries long dead.

The Singing Sword

I dreamt my love went flying
To realms both far and free;
Such storms we're meant to weather,
The two of us together,
Yet still I went out sighing
Across that cold dark sea.
I dreamt my love went flying
To realms both far and free.

And so I followed after,
To seek her in that air.
I traveled rivers swollen
By spells both grim and olden,
A place that absent laughter,
Held trees all sparse and bare.
And so I followed after,
To seek her in that air.

Hippolite

Its king was dark and evil,
His throne was built of brass.
His subjects cringed while kneeling;
To him there's no appealing,
Most cruel and most medieval
His harshness none surpass.
Its king was dark and evil,
His throne is built of brass.

His queen sat rigid, stolid,
And yet I knew her well!
It was she and no other,
She had become his lover;
She seemed a ghost, not solid—
Dear God, what awful spell!
His queen sat rigid, stolid,
And yet I knew her well!

I begged and then I pleaded,
And wept there like a child.
The two of them unmoving,
My love was nothing proving,
My words all went unheeded;
I was most frantic, wild.
I begged and then I pleaded,
And wept there like a child.

They mocked me with their laughter,
Reviled me with their scorn.
I prayed then to our Savior,

For change in this behavior;
Then something shook each rafter,
The walls were cracked and torn.
They mocked me with their laughter,
Reviled me with their scorn.

A sword came at me flying;
I grabbed its hilt and swung.
I struck that king while screaming,
And cursing all his scheming!
He bellowed in his dying,
My singing sword had sung!
A sword came at me flying;
I grabbed its hilt and swung.

I took my dreaming lover;
We fled that place, fled fast!
Through Space we wandered lonely
Through realms obscure, unholy;
Our own we would discover,
There at the very last.
I took my dreaming lover;
We fled that place, fled fast!

I'm with my lover ever,
Here where we both belong.
We trade both love and kisses,
The rarest love, yes, this is,
And none may now dissever
Us two from dawn till dawn!

I'm with my lover ever,
Here where we both belong.

The Witches' Château

I found that grotto where once long ago
I held your hand to greet the new dawn's heat.
And still, withal, that time, how swift and fleet!
A mile or more beyond that grim château,
Where legend said the winter witches go,
You whispered then, and smiled: "It's their retreat."
And then I kissed those lips of yours, most sweet,
As dawn fell on that ancient cold plateau.

And now, in retrospect, as we kissed there,
You'd chance a look to where the witches rest.
I thought it fear, yes, fear, and thought it best
To spin you round and feel your flowing hair.
Then you rose in the dark, as light as foam,
Bid me goodbye, then flew off to your home.

1934

I walk this night along the spellbound shore.
The wind through caves went whispering, and told
A tale of lost and smuggled pirate gold,
As I stand here in nineteen thirty-four.

Their long ships in the surf, the tide's huge roar
Drowns out their voices in the midnight cold;
And cutthroats all, long since their souls have sold,
They place their loot, the gold, in caves to store.

They spy me and I stare in abject fear.
With cutlass and with pistol storm the beach,
But then I watch them as they disappear,
As I am wakened by a lone gull's screech.
I move down past the entrance of a cave,
Mark well the pirates and my unmarked grave.

The Forsaken City

In cities forsaken,
    In deserts grown sere,
At dawn I awaken,
    At dawn I appear!

These stone columns fluted,
    All cracked and they tilt.
This ghost city's muted
    And never rebuilt.

I move through its alleys
    Long drifted with sand.
These stars like strange galleys
    That none may command.

Near mall and bordello
> The old stage is set.
Its stones have turned yellow,
> Its ghosts know regret.

I once knew a slattern,
> Both comely and sweet—
That sad daily pattern
> Of girls of the street.

Both lovely and graceful
> And kind as a child,
Was always most tasteful,
> And yet could be wild.

For years I would meet her
> Out under these stars.
I'd kiss her, then greet her—
> Ah, such love was ours.

Yet sad was the dawning
> That struck like a knife,
When under this awning,
> She ended her life.

The night wind still whispers;
> The brothel is gone.
And so are her sisters,
> To oblivion.

Through cities forsaken
    By eagle and kite,
With regret am I taken
    And weep through the night.

I Sigh to Orion

Far west of forever I fly on the breeze
    And sigh to Orion at dusk.
The cup of lost love I have drained to the lees
As I bank and I soar above cold haunted seas,
    My sole guide is the moon's well-honed tusk.

I dream of my lovers long dead and supine
    That sank long ago in these seas.
I pray to the one God these stars may align,
For I know that I'm here through some ancient design,
    Yet I waste away here by degrees.

I hang like a gull on this briny sea air
    While my heart is a furnace of pain.
I'm a skip and jump from the realm of despair,
I look for redemption yet no one is there.
    My life was a tale most arcane.

I mark a dead seaport whose castles are bleak
    And ruined with dark weathered stone;
And here I descend for some succor to seek,
I shamble down hallways destroyed and unique,
    Where only these ghost winds now drone.

I leisurely leap from these bluffs in a trice
    And I soar by the light of these stars.
It goes without saying I've paid a great price;
My sins are twice dark and of evil device,
    More crimson than is scarlet Mars.

Far west of forever I fly on the breeze,
    And sigh to Orion at dusk.
The cup of lost love I have drained to the lees
As I bank and I soar above cold haunted seas,
    My sole guide is the moon's well-honed tusk.

In Upland Fields

I dream of realms most lonely
    In outré nightmare lands,
Of islands grim, unholy,
    On black volcanic sands.

Here hulking idols tower
    While in their restless shade
Wild orchids, teeming, flower,
    As ghosts file in parade.

Beyond the ruined city
    Gray werewolves stalk abroad;
Remorseless, without pity,
    They give those idols laud.

Hard on those blackened beaches,
    Above the foaming tide,
A frightened gull now screeches
    Where rolling sea mists glide.

It's here I court disaster
    Whenever nightmares call,
To flee these shores the faster
    Ere comes the nightmare squall.

It's inland to the mountains,
    Through upland fields of grain,
Past ruined granite fountains,
    To cross the haunted plain.

The ferns and gnarled trees thicken,
    And danger stalks the way;
This land is haunted, stricken.
    It's here the werewolves stray.

I met a green-eyed harlot—
    She's leaner than a rail.
Her thick and long hair scarlet,
    Her flesh so deathly pale.

As lovely as a goddess,
    In some sense seemed a child;
With silk embroidered bodice,
    Her eyes were savage, wild.

She led me through the brambles
    Past fallen temples there,
An awful ancient shambles,
    Across a flagstone square.

We wandered through a valley,
    Around an antique pile,
And down some haunted alley
    We went mile after mile.

So fast my heart was beating,
    I knew we were near dawn,
This dream most swift and fleeting,
    I woke and it was gone.

The Ghost, the Gold, and the Dark

I fight the cold
While buried gold
Lies on the hillside there.
Here from the coast
Each ragged ghost
Will haunt me in this air.

I come alone,
It is foreknown
That gold among these oaks
Is buried deep
Where dead men sleep,
Wrapped in their tattered cloaks.

Orion looms
Above their tombs
Beyond this frozen stream,
Yet still I go
To this plateau,
As in some haunted dream.

Who would have thought
Despair had caught
Me in this tangled web,
Until this eve
When I perceive
My life will wane and ebb?

And now I climb
Through frost and slime
To reach that copse of trees,
And death I smell,
The breath of hell
Is wafted on the breeze.

I'll come not back
This awful track
That leads me to the coast,
For now alway
It's here I stay,
A pale and dreary ghost.

Down to the Sea in Ships

Secluded Bays

On islands with secluded bays
Where rusting ships remain as wrecks,
It's here observers I'll amaze
And make them gape and strain their necks.

For I'm a spirit far from home
Who haunts the coves and headlands there;
I'm insubstantial as sea foam
And vanish into thinnest air.

At dusk I watch the comets storm,
Each pale as any seaborne ghost,
While some presage a future harm
To ships along this rock bound coast.

I sleep within this coral reef;
Out of the surf I spool at dawn,
Recall with sorrow mine old grief,
Then like the sea breeze I am gone.

Across these rusting freighters I
Will frighten sea birds as I go;
Then soar into that midnight sky,
Then out across the long plateau.

On islands with secluded bays
Where rusting ships remain as wrecks,
It's here observers I'll amaze
And make them gape and strain their necks.

These Haunted Hills I Roam

Down through the halls of tireless Time
    I sped there all alone,
There as the bronze bells clang and chime,
    In towers of gleaming stone.

Here, where the typhoon floods and sweeps
    The headland and lagoon,
Is where my ashen lover weeps
    Under an iron moon.

Ah, give me the key of Time to quell
    This pain that will not leave!
And give me a sword to break this spell
    That shamans harshly weave.

Give me my lover in skirts of silk,
    Her lips as tart as rum,
And give me more girls of her soft ilk
    In torques of platinum!

Over these haunted hills I roam,
    My steed is lathered so,
And down to the breaker's frothing foam
    Is where this eve I go.

Lucinda with your eyes of gray,
    Come let me soothe your pain.
I'll sail my fleets from this sad bay
    To Singapore or Spain.

Down through the halls of tireless Time
    I sped there all alone,
There as the bronze bells clang and chime
    In towers of gleaming stone.

The Drowning

Now but a ghost sometimes I deeply dredge
The cold lake's bottom in a fruitless search;
With pale and ghostly hands I sift and lurch
All up its sloping banks and through the sedge.
Sometimes I dream, on some forgotten ledge
Within the lake she's found a secret perch,
A place I long to find, like some still church,
And find it yet I will—this is my pledge!

But should I not despair that she is gone?
Her spirit does not flinch before the rod
Of loneliness from dusk until the dawn,
With blows as I do. She has gone to God
And I am left to grieve, my heart a stone,
To haunt this icy lake by night, alone.

Under an Iron Moon

Under the eye of an iron moon
    I stood my sentry post,
Hard by this haunted strange lagoon,
    Along this savage coast.

And the stars rose up and outward spread
    Under this iron moon,
Here where the ancient long-drowned dead
    Swim in this dark lagoon.

And some of these ghosts are pale and fleet,
    Some are as slow as mud;
Some are swift and light on their feet
    With hair as red as blood.

These are the girls that charm me so,
    Whistle a girlish tune;
They splash up when the tide is low
    Under this iron moon.

I feel a love for their scarlet hair,
    And one young girl the most;
She'll stay with me in this frigid air,
    A most enchanting ghost.

And she talks of love and boys long dead,
    Here in the frigid cold;
So pretty the hair on her scarlet head,
    Which warrants a crown of gold.

As the dawn draws near we each will sigh,
    Our words become jejune;
And the light goes dim out of the sky
    That comes from the iron moon.

And never a care shall come to me,
> Here as I guard this shore,
For I was drowned in this haunted sea
> That I guard forevermore!

The Viking Horn

Come harken to horns that have hammered and hound
> Me forever past lost silver streams.
They blare on this coast and awaken the drowned,
And they call up dead kings both crowned and uncrowned,
> They echo throughout all my dreams.

Like Vikings of old on the prow of some ship,
> A dragon ship now to be sure,
They blow on brass horns till there's blood on the lip,
As that dragon ship's launched right out of its slip
> Where the tide is a loud rushing roar!

In valleys of dream where I wander alone,
> I see a pale love but for me;
Yet I hear those damned horns, be they brass or white bone—
They sound in my dream like Leviathan's groan,
> Ere he comes up out of the sea!

I hide in a cave down a seldom-trod trail,
> To sleep with a nymph that I know.
With our hands to our ears we yet hear that loud wail
And curse those dead Vikings, this dream and this tale,
> For in dreams I have nowhere to go!

I climb to the top of a wind-blasted tor,
    Where the only sound is the storm.
This place of all places, it has its allure—
I'm away from mad horns that sound on the shore
    And at length I'm free from their harm!

Come harken to horns that have hammered and hound
    Me forever past lost silver streams.
They blare on this coast and awaken the drowned,
And they call up dead kings both crowned and uncrowned,
    They echo throughout all my dreams.

Rendezvous

I sail here as these shadows fade
    Around me near the lake;
I mark the stars, a vast parade,
    And wish the dead to wake;
The dead are dead and well decayed,
    And so my heart will ache.

And from my boat I see displayed,
    Just past the reedy brake,
Where she, alone, is deeply laid
    And mark her ghost opaque.
I come ashore now unafraid,
    Our rendezvous to make!

For her I'd lead some great crusade,
    Although my heart should quake;
Vast legions I would slay, invade,
    Her hand once more to take.
Her ghost stands near the colonnade:
    Her love I'll not forsake!

Song of the Sea Dog's Ghost

I'm a son of the sea and a savage lad—
My enemies stuck on my lance's gad!
And ever I roam where the bitter spume
Blows in my face from a growing gale,
With my shipmates and I now courting doom,
Under a huge and billowing sail!

I'm a son of the sea and a savage man—
My earring was looted in Isfahan,
My women are harlots of lowly cast,
Who crowd these wharfs when we come ashore
To sate our lust grown awful and vast:
They love my cursing and bellowing roar!

I'm a son of the sea and savage rake—
These pretty girls' hearts and men's backs I break!
And I love to fight when the sun is high,
And yet one stout rover he made me squeal,
For he pierced my heart and there I would die
By his cutlass of polished and well-honed steel!

Now my ghost it haunts these coasts and the bays—
I ever regret my wicked old ways
And haunt all the girls and all of the men
That late at night in their warm beds lie;
I haunt them ever and ever, again,
To vanish at dawn with a savage sigh.

I'm a son of the sea and a savage lad—
My enemies stuck on my lance's gad!
And ever I roam where the bitter spume
Blows in my face from a growing gale,
With my shipmates and I now courting doom,
Under a huge and billowing sail!

One Misty Morn

One misty morn I sat
When fog hung thin and pale,
Upon the cliff top's grassy mat
And thought I saw a sail:
Rectangular that canvas flapped.
The waves seemed lavender;
This vision all my vigor sapped,
My soul began to stir.

I could not see the boat beneath,
Yet saw its silver mast:
The boat snug in a misty sheath,
That sailed upon the vast.

The Silent Sea

I felt that Time had slipped apace,
That sail moved on the deep.
The mist seemed like fine tatted lace—
And then I fell asleep.

Beguiled

Out of the surf, out of the sand, I drew
The lacquered lamp. Its fine and arching spout
Was worked with silver sigils used as grout,
Full tinted with a cerulean blue.
My heart, an iron anvil, whispered this:
"O genius of the lamp, if such you are,
Come forth, fire this dark heart like some bright star,
Or steer me to wolf-headed Anubis!"

And she came forth, her almond eyes so wide,
Her elfin form with flesh like cinnabar.
So close, so close she stood there at my side.
The two of us alone on that sandbar;
"I will instruct you now," she purred and smiled:
She took my hand; I am beguiled, beguiled.

In the Moonlight

A Siren with the smoothest skin
Bathes in this tidal pool at noon.
Shy suitors dream her love to win
At dusk below the sickle moon.

She combs her hair of ebony
With her small comb of polished horn.
The moonlight with its ivory
Will her pale flesh at dusk adorn.

Her suitors in the shadows sigh
And dream their boyish dreams once more,
That they may with this Siren lie
Upon this lone fantastic shore.

Iron and Silver

Iron and silver and jewels from the sea
Beckon, seduce, and they call out to me!
Far past these mountains
One iron rung bell
Tolls near the fountains
Down deep in this dell.

Wine and base women are all that I know—
Would it were else, and my soul pure as snow!
Yet all that I gain
And all that I keep
Rings me with pain
And robs me of sleep!

Shrive my sins ever, and lead me away,
Down past the rivers, and down to the bay!
Wash me in waters

Refreshing and cool,
While Poseidon's daughters
Call me a fool!

Sea Shanty

My heart is for one who is deep and cool,
    And old as the stars above.
She's clean and strong and an elegant jewel,
    My one and eternal love.

Stalwart she is, and a beauty so vast
    Beyond where the eye can see.
Now both day and night, and both first and last
    I give my heart to the sea.

I'm wrapped in her arms when I'm caught in her swells,
    As ever a lover might be.
When I smell the spume and I hear a ship's bells,
    I'm with her again, the sea!

Her wet wild ways, be they narrow or wide,
    Will always be home to me.
With my true love would I ever abide
    And pledge my troth to the sea!

When I run on the storm in the grim typhoon,
    Or gales on the Zuider Zee,
When the hurricane erases the moon,
    Even then I will love the sea.

For am I so fickle a lover as this,
    That under a storm I should flee?
But even so stricken I'd beg a last kiss,
    Then go down to rest in the sea!

Harold Owen Confronts His Brother's Ghost*

The sea was roiled with foam; the air was thick;
And there I saw my brother in the room,
In candlelight. His eyes were fraught with gloom,
While staring forward past the candlestick.
I thought perhaps it was some fake, a trick
By some unseen magician. Strange perfume,
An otherworldly essence dripping doom,
Now wounded my poor heart and made me sick.

Ramrod straight he sat, clutched his riding crop;
He seemed to manage just the barest smile.
I tried to greet him—something made me stop;
I stood and stared for quite a long, long while.
I learned, days later, a grief I must confront,
His ghost had traveled from the Western Front.

*On Armistice Day, November 11, 1918 (the day World War I ended), Harold Owen, a British naval officer and the younger brother of the poet Wilfred Owen, was on board the HMS Astraea off the coast of South Africa when he saw the ghost of his brother sitting in his stateroom. It was not until several days later that he learned that his brother had died in France on November 4th.

Leviathan

I dreamt he plunged again into the deep
And took me and my ship of thin rattan.
A titan fish of eighty cubits' span,
And made me toss and turn within my sleep.
He angled downward, most swiftly and twice steep
Near ancient coasts of shogun-ruled Japan,
As faster sped this dark Leviathan;
Such terrors would I lean and sadly reap.

I woke up with a start, all drenched in sweat.
The moon swung high, the sea wind blew a gale;
The landscape shivered darkly, shot with gray.
I shook with unknown fears, and knew regret—
And then it was I went weak and turned pale
For there I saw him, splashing in the bay!

The Matilda

To starboard, to homeward my frigate will tack.
    Through sea mist will all things now seem
Occluded and foreign and shadowed in black,
As the lines of my rigging have loosened from slack,
    While I chart my course here through this dream.

My ghostly pale crew, both alert and austere,
    They attend to my slightest command,
Where I stand at the helm and I patiently steer.

I wait for far mountains to rise and appear
    And anxiously wait to sight land.

The swell of this sea is a silent sad song
    That haunts me as waves slap my hull.
I pray to our God that it may not be long
That we see both the land and the scarlet of dawn,
    Instead of this wan moon's pale skull.

I sail the *Matilda*—she's named for my wife—
    Through a dark and relentless cold storm.
I long to be home and away from this strife,
For longing's a savage and sharp-bladed knife!
    How I long to be rescued from harm!

Yet we sail and we sail through these ages grown vast;
    Our desire no other may slake.
We sail toward the Future from out of the Past,
Yet we'll voyage along right down to the last,
    Until from this nightmare I wake.

To starboard, to homeward my frigate will tack.
    Through sea mist will all things now seem
Occluded and foreign and shadowed in black,
As the lines of my rigging have loosened from slack,
    While I chart my course through this dream.

Bethany

Things never were as they might seem:
    Lost is that key
That could unlock my darkest dream
    Of Bethany.

She was a girl that all men sought:
    Such anarchy,
She made it clear she could be bought,
    Did Bethany.

So many men like to a horde
    Would pay her fee;
Reviled by some, yet most adored,
    Sweet Bethany.

Her hair was sometimes black, or red,
    Groomed strikingly.
I think perhaps her soul was dead?
    Poor Bethany.

Her pretty mouth would laugh and curse.
    With rancor she
Would claim her lovers were far worse
    Than Bethany.

And truth to tell she had not erred;
    For truthfully
She could be vile, yet she was scared,
    Was Bethany.

She seemed completely in control:
    Assuredly
Her work would take an awful toll
    On Bethany.

Whatever joy she had, had fled,
    Drowned in some sea,
Reserved there for the living dead,
    Like Bethany.

I told her then, a thousand times,
    That she should flee—
That I'd go with her to far climes,
    With Bethany.

She laughed and smiled; her pretty face,
    Disturbingly,
Turned white as I would then embrace
    My Bethany.

So many nights I sought her there
    Relentlessly.
I was in love. She could not care,
    Could Bethany.

Love was like a shining dream
    That could not be,
A ghost or chimera would seem
    To Bethany.

Love was Atlantis, or far Mu,
    Mere fantasy.
Its truth she could not then construe,
    Sad Bethany.

Now forty years have passed, and still,
    Half sleepily,
I dream I'm with her on a hill,
    With Bethany.

She smiles and says she now knows joy
    Here by this sea;
She says that love all ills destroy,
    Oh, Bethany!

Xardoc Ibrahim

Lost love I sought here to redeem
With charms and conjured beings fell,
Or some Time-lost, Phoenician spell,
Above my brazier's swirling steam.

My magic tome so dark, extreme:
I mouthed the words but few have said,
To call back from the ancient dead
The wizard Xardoc Ibrahim.

Within Time's fabric, one fine seam,
I pulled the wizard through to me.
Here in my keep, hard by the sea,
Stood now that sorcerer supreme!

He wore a woolen robe of cream;
Upon it gilded cuneiform
Glared at me as through some twisted storm
While his blue eyes were all agleam.

"Ah, fool," he cried, "I see your scheme!
Little it is of use to me!
I'll see you drowned within this sea
To serve in Neptune's cold regime!"

Now all to me is as a dream:
I toil where sharks and blind rays dwell
Within this deep and icy hell,
Dispatched by Xardoc Ibrahim.

A Dark Dream of the Sea

In dreams I go under
    The swell of the sea,
Then under and under
    Gigantically!
Then down to the dreary
    Wreck of a ship
Where bones of the weary
    Still slide and slip.

The thunder is raging,
    As the buoy bell
Now rings as if paging
    There in the swell;

And I'm brought here lonely
    As ever a child
To this place most unholy,
    Tragic, and wild!

Hard by the headland
    Dragoons call to me
Out of some dead land
    Out of the sea!
The pale moon is frowning
    Up there in the sky
While here I am drowning
    In silt where I lie!

In dreams I go under
    The swell of the sea,
Then under and under
    Gigantically!
Then down to the dreary
    Wreck of a ship
Where bones of the weary
    Still slide and slip.

Sea Magic

Under these stars in a sable sky
These tidal pools at low tide lie,
    Where moon shadows cover half these pools.
    The mermaids' eyes all shine like jewels,

And the dark is filled with song and sigh
    As the cool wind eddies, moans and spools
And the moon glows bright with her silver eye,
    As then at length she begins to set
    The night grows dark as polished jet.

Now over the waves a mermaid's coo,
Her eyes flash fire in cobalt blue;
    There on that midnight and haunted shore,
    She weaves with song a dark glamour,
As magics abound and now accrue,
    To charm my heart with a deep allure.
Stars wink on with an amber hue;
    I feel wet hands as they pull and tug,
    Know a matchless, watery hug.

The Ferryman

On darkling eves stupendous and most drear,
I walk alone by ghost lights through this fen;
I've come here through the werewolf-haunted glen,
Past iron gods with each a wicked sneer.
I've heard some great demonian dark gear
Go grinding grist, and grinding it again,
Until I feel cut off from other men
As odd stars in this sky will now appear.

At length I reach the river bank and there
It seems I see dark Charon and his boat;

While I can scarcely breathe this humid air,
I try to speak, yet something's in my throat.
Then in that boatman's eyes I see a glare,
He speaks to me: "Fret not, I have your fare!"

The Schooner

My love is like a schooner
That plies a stormy sea.
I deftly man the tiller
To calm and then to still her;
Now later or then sooner
I fight her sorcery.
My love is like a schooner
That plies a stormy sea.

I trim her sails and steer her
Beyond the deadly reef.
Sometimes she is so eager,
My strength seems useless, meager;
It's then she is the dearer,
Yet sometimes leads to grief.
I trim her sails and steer her
Beyond the deadly reef.

For years I have been sailing,
Yet she's the rarest jewel:
She's small and frail, yet agile,
Both sturdy and still fragile.

Sometimes I fear she's ailing;
In truth she's often cruel.
For years I have been sailing,
Yet she's the rarest jewel.

My love is like a schooner
That plies a stormy sea.
I deftly man the tiller
To calm and then to still her,
Now later or then sooner
I fight her sorcery.
My love is like a schooner
That plies a stormy sea.

The Vanished Sea

Across the shifted sand the night breeze flies.
Ghosts deep beneath the gray and pockmarked stone
Send up a whispering and eerie moan,
And when the twilight comes they start to rise.
Long shadows in their huge and eyeless eyes,
And yellowed is each desiccated bone,
And I am here, abandoned and alone,
For here is where my broken body lies.

I fumble through this sand where once the coast
Of that long-vanished saline inland sea.
I wander aimlessly a pallid ghost,

Yet from this desert I may never flee.
So nights I haunt this wadi and these graves,
The distant dunes out to the cliffside caves.

Above the Bay in Rajapore

I have seen the eagle soar
Above the bay in Rajapore,
And I have drifted down the Nile
With Asha in a deep sopor
Past banks where hunts the crocodile.

In some tall mountain's snowy tor
I hear the haunted oceans roar,
And I have traveled mile on mile
To seek a Siren on the shore
Whose brilliant eyes brim full of guile.

Through snake-infested fens I take
The trail that leads down to the brake
Where ruins of a massive pile
Lay sunken in the silent lake,
And I have loitered there awhile.

In cloud cities where they make
Weapons all the world to shake,
I quick escaped with Asha there
Through realms dark magics will remake,
To drink the wine that slakes despair.

Deep in canyons dry and red,
Under clouds as dark as lead,
I've builded citadels of gneiss,
And my sweet Asha there I wed
And learned the power of her kiss.

On other rivers we have sailed,
Heedless when our craft was hailed,
Down through the jungles of the South,
Nor has my burning love once failed
To kiss the flower of her mouth.

Sea Ghosts and Shipwrecks

Sea ghosts and shipwrecks are rife with their grief,
And hide in the sea mist above this white reef.
Ever at twilight
Under these stars
With the moon's highlight
Presaging red Mars.

Sea ghosts and shipwrecks, forgotten old schemes,
This bay a doorway to lost plundered dreams.
While up on these beaches
The gray shadows strain,
As each one now reaches
This long low moraine.

Sea ghosts and shipwrecks all full of allure
As I wait here at twilight for my paramour,
She comes from these tides,
And it's always for me,
By daylight abides
Down deep in this sea.

Mount Carmel by the Sea

I hear the call of abbey bells
That broke my heart and saddened me,
One mile across these ocean's swells,
Upon Mount Carmel by the Sea.

Those cloister walls, of granite made,
Now wall her from the world and me.
For many months now she has prayed
Upon Mount Carmel by the Sea.

Those bells sometimes a serenade,
Sometimes as cruel as they can be.
The call of God none may evade
Upon Mount Carmel by the Sea.

Those bells so like a hardened thief,
At matins I can hear their plea.
My petty love has turned to grief
Upon Mount Carmel by the Sea.

I hear the call of abbey bells
That now no longer saddens me,
One mile across these ocean's swells,
Upon Mount Carmel by the Sea.

A Shipman's Dream

Down in the trough my ship will climb
    As sea-spray mists the deck and mast,
In icy weather turns to rime,
    As tall waves inky shadows cast.

That salt sea air is biting yet,
    Deep in my dreams or when I wake.
My only longing, my regret—
    The wheel once more my hands to take!

To feel the ship beneath my feet
    And hear the gulls' most raucous caw;
Against my face the storm-blown sleet,
    To feel her pitch, to feel her yaw!

Now four leagues from a sheltered bay
    I'd steer her true before the storm.
Ah, what I'd give for one more day
    Away from home that's safe and warm!

The Witch of the West

The witch of the West woos, winnowing lovers
    At dawn in this witch-haunted lea.
She seeks a lover like none of the others,
Her love's obsessive, it crushes and smothers,
    As she waits for him here by this sea.

Her name is Lucasta, a tall luscious girl,
    Who seems to be scarcely a teen.
Yet she's old as the world as she'll playfully swirl
One long lock of hair that she'll twirl and she'll twirl;
    While she's pretty, her evil's unseen.

She sits on a stone. It's an old carven bench—
    It was made by a craftsman of old.
She waits in the rain which will thoroughly drench
The black silken robes of this pale lusting wench,
    Who adorns her small ears with fine gold.

The moon rises up and the rain ceases then,
    And she dries her wet cloths with a word.
The air is now charged with the stench of the fen,
The grave of her lovers, all half-rotted men,
    While she whistles like some timid bird.

Now the earl's second son appears on the verge
    Of the hill that will lead up to her.
Then out of the mist, like a ghost he'll emerge.
Her dark heart now beats with an unquenchable urge—
    She feels the old lust again stir.

She takes his warm hand and she rises to kiss
    The lips of her new royal beau;
And she smiles at the thought of expected new bliss,
Yet she knows she'll soon tire of him and of this—
    Like a ghost all her pleasure will go.

The witch of the West woos, winnowing lovers
    At dawn in this witch-haunted lea.
She seeks a lover like none of the others,
Her love's obsessive, it crushes and smothers,
    As she waits for him here by this sea.

Calypso

I dreamt Calypso lured me to her cave,
A slender girl, exceptional and tall.
She wore a mesh and silken see-through shawl
And very little else; her aspect grave.
She smiled and made me seem, somehow, most brave,
Then led me down a long and columned hall,
Into a chamber rich, imperial;
She made me then her base, unwilling slave.

Unlike Ulysses, lacking all his strength,
Nor half his mighty wit did I possess;
She used me badly there, and then at length
I left behind that lovely sorceress,
And with dispatch I ended all my strife.
Then sailed through storms to my unhappy wife.

The Dark Girl

Night's now never a girl of favor,
    Under the moon's impressive ark.
Only the lost may sigh to savor
    This fay child of the shadowed dark.
She walks with me to the skiff that's waiting,
Wearing the moon like silver plating,
Into the boat, then navigating
    Across this lake in a wooden barque.

Fay and frail, and a fickle lover,
    We come ashore hard by these yews.
Taste the poisoned honey of her,
    Mesmerized by her dream-sung coos.
The werewolves' cry so long and pealing,
Locked in her arms my head now reeling;
Now like a drunkard, weeping, kneeling,
    Lost to her who so deftly woos.

Cold and listless there in the shallows,
    She watches from the nearby brake.
Her presence all this place unhallows;
    My heart and soul she means to take!
Never now the sky's blue awning,
Nor will I watch the brilliant dawning,
Rather my ghost will shriek while fawning
    Upon her at dusk by this cold lake!

The Ship

Cold the call of the west wind's whistle,
    Snow and sleet on the high seas grind;
Sharp is the wind's prick, like a thistle,
    Lone on the waves, no help to find.
Stronger now is that storm wind growing,
From out of hell that gale now blowing;
The wearied crew alert and knowing,
    Death grows near as they're sailing blind.

Under this vault of heaven reeling,
    The death ships sinks now by her stern,
With each moment her fate fast sealing,
    More angrily now the dark waves churn.
Her bow comes up in anguished fashion;
Her worn-out crew wide-eyed and ashen,
Down she sinks in her final passion,
    Marked by the flight of a lonesome erne.

Six Days out of Zanzibar

I've seen the sanguine stars collide
    Above the maelstrom as the call
From my too pale and vanished bride
    Whispers her ghostly madrigal.

Once in a distant port of call
    A ghost appeared beyond the rail;

'Twas winter then in Portugal,
    When there I saw that spectral sail.

That ghost ship held me there in thrall;
    I saw her long and streaming hair.
She stood so wan and magical,
    And floated in that twilight air.

I saw her twirl her parasol.
    My ship hung on a large sandbar,
In far climes equatorial,
    Six days out of Zanzibar.

Once past the gleaming cliffs of Spain
    When storm-clouds hung funereal,
I questioned what was real and sane—
    She stood there hulking, colossal!

I've seen the sanguine stars collide
    Above the maelstrom as the call
From my too pale and vanished bride
    Whispers her ghostly madrigal.

Conversion

In Antioch the ships come in
And moor against each granite dock,
And here run harlots young and thin
    In Antioch.

Each traveler will slowly walk,
Each proffered some warm, tempting sin,
Pulled nearly to the brothels' block.

Paul meets them, yet not with chagrin,
Is happy to confer and talk
With many lovely souls to win
    In Antioch.

A Dream of Leviathan

Leviathan rose in my dream
With mottled flesh of black and tan,
His purblind eyes a sallow cream,
    Leviathan.

Down in the bay dark ripples fan,
The water roils and turns to steam;
There's something there to threaten man.

Asleep, again one wan moonbeam
Slides through my shutter of rattan,
And still I hear my echoed scream—
    Leviathan!

Bell Isle

I heard the far-off iron isle bells rung.
At once so like a distant screech and moan,
They seemed to call the pylons and the stone
From Bronze Age cairns when all the earth was young.
The heavy iron clapper, that loud tongue,
Was heard above the rest, its magic thrown
Upon the brewing storm-wind and was blown
To lands that weep from constant sorrow sung.

I stood upon the cliff face and my eyes
Were filled with salty brine not of the sea.
I heard the sad and dreary linnets' cries
Flung on the wind and then forced back to me.
I marveled at the ancient evil spells
That rang out with those ghostly iron bells.

By the Haunted Sea

I watch when winter storms will gather
    Beyond this bay that is my home,
And there the crashing seas will lather
    As white as snow and pale as foam.
Then in my room I mark her spindle
As shadows now both lengthen, dwindle,
    While memories old thoughts rekindle,
Though she sleeps in the frozen loam.

I watch the dim wraiths floating, ashen.
    I think of her who was so fair,
Rekindled now mine ancient passion;
    It seems I sense her scented hair.
Red embers in my hearth are glowing;
Outside a haunted wind is blowing,
With everything about me slowing,
    I see her shimmer on the air!

She's now before me standing, sighing.
    She moves with such agility,
Her golden hair cascading, flying,
    Pure beauty, yet fragility.
And by some great miracle is loaned,
While all my senses she has honed,
Renewed again the love we owned
    Hard by this chilling, haunted sea.

I Heard Swift Ghostly Fingers

I heard swift ghostly fingers on the frets
Of fairy-builded ancient mandolins,
A music that might lave away all sins,
Renew lost love and nullify regrets.
I marked wan ghosts upon these parapets
Like angels dancing on the heads of pins,
Voices ethereal, like violins;
Upon that air the scent of anisettes.

* * *

My heart was hooked, as with some angel's gaff.
I sought to storm those parapets to find
A burning love that is divine, the staff
Of life itself, a covenant to bind
My heart and soul hard by this ancient sea
For now, and for all of eternity.

The Trysting Place

At the sea's soft edge where the broad bay beckons
    Where the star-streams gather in fog and mist,
The ghost of a pale girl nightly reckons
    That this hour of night is fixed for her tryst.
Her Asian hair, like the night, falls silky,
    To cover her shoulders in greater part.
Like sea-foam her face is soft and milky;
    She hides her heart.

With such grace she moves through the shallows wading;
    The curve of each leg is full of allure.
This headland's cliff in this moonlight is shading
    Her pretty form and this part of the shore.
Only the song of the sea now to charm her,
    Strong ghostly echoes here rise to the sky;
She seeks for a lover to hold and warm her:
    At dawn she'll die.

She splashes out quickly, there from the waters;
    Hails me in words that are unknown to me.
Like the youngest of all of Neptune's fine daughters,
    She thinks me her lover, a son of the sea.
Then in a moment we're greedily holding
    Our bodies so tightly that neither now breathes!
This pretty pale girl in my own arms I'm folding—
    My heart seethes and seethes!

So long are these nights she passes, waiting,
    Here where these wet rocks so darkly gleam.
Never a lover to come to her sating
    All of her wishes, for this is her dream.
I move to her there, my right hand waving,
    Her pretty faced flushed, no longer wan;
Thinks I'm her lover, she basks in the saving—
    Then she is gone.

At the sea's soft edge where the broad bay beckons
    Where the star-streams gather in fog and mist,
The ghost of a pale girl nightly reckons
    That this hour of night is fixed for her tryst.
Her Asian hair, like the night, falls silky,
    To cover her shoulders in greater part.
Like sea-foam her face is soft and milky;
    She hides her heart.

Windward and Lee

Winter and lashings
Both windward and lee;
Tides with their bashings
Roil all of the sea,
And I watch as the gulls in such terror flee.

Cloud heads and surges
Portending the storm;
Waves like great scourges
Bring ruin and harm,
Yet I stand in a place here safe from its harm.

Moon tides and thunder,
With echoes obscure,
Fill me with wonder
On this haunted shore;
I dream of my sweet and most pale paramour.

Seawalls and headlands,
The bay and its reef,
All seeming dead lands,
Set off in relief.
My heart's been purloined by a lovely wan thief.

Winter and rumbles
Of storms as they wane;
Whispers and grumbles
Make known my sharp pain,
As I float here till dawn with the numberless slain.

Seven Sisters

A song is in the whispers
>That ghosts lisp on the breeze.
These seven ghostly sisters
>Haunt caves hard by the seas.

Their song is most alluring,
>Enough to make men swoon,
So ghostly and enduring
>Below this amber moon.

A song is in the whispers
>As combers crash ashore.
I see those seven sisters
>Who through the sea-caves soar.

Their beauty most disturbing;
>Their eyes deep drowning pools.
My soul they are perturbing—
>They've garnered many fools!

A song is in the whispers
>When dusk is on the land.
Those willowy wan sisters
>Reach out to grasp my hand.

The nearest one is glowing
>And stares at me quite bold.
Her scarlet hair is flowing
>While her sisters' hair is gold.

A song is in the whispers,
    It hangs upon the air,
As each of seven sisters
    Is combing out her hair.

Their combs are white and pretty,
    Their kisses all men crave.
These sisters have no pity
    And lure me to their cave.

A song is in the whispers
    That rise up from the sea,
Sung by these seven sisters
    Who now have captured me.

Love Uncanny

My love is uncanny,
    Directed at thee,
Intense and twice manly,
    As strong as the sea!
My purpose most loyal,
    A strong iron rod,
For thou art a royal
    Creation of God.

My heart is a feather
    That wafts with the breeze,
In fair or foul weather,
    Across savage seas.

I move with thy sighing
    Near each rocky shore,
With eagles I'm vying
    Behind and before.

I'll battle all urges
    That keep us apart,
Then wait till love surges
    Right out of my heart!
I'll soar with strong breezes
    And fly with the loons,
My strength as the sea's is,
    My love glowing moons!

Thy love is a tether
    That we never part,
And yet there's no measure
    To measure my heart.
Nocturnal, diurnal,
    My love is the same
And ever eternal
    My heart is aflame!

I burn with such fire
    Now unendingly
And full of desire,
    Yet only for thee!
I cull from the heavens
    The vastness of stars.
My love seeks and leavens
    All that is ours!

I'll give thee fair cities
    All teeming with gold,
And delicate pretties
    To have and to hold,
And orchids of magic
    That grow on the moors,
Give thee songs tragic
    Of young troubadours.

I'll dance with you under
    These gray shadowed walls
And fill you with wonder
    At masquerade balls!
And then in the gloaming
    We'll watch this cool sea,
Whose breakers are foaming
    There eternally!

My kingdoms I offer,
    My ships I give thee;
My heart I now proffer,
    Here hard by this sea.
Strong love that's unending,
    With kisses galore,
My will that's unbending,
    For thee on this shore!

Take all of me, lover,
    And hammer my will.
My love you'll discover
    In waters most still.

My arms will surround thee
    Like great walls of gneiss;
My love is around thee,
    I die for your kiss!

My sword am I wielding
    Both near and so far;
My love now unyielding—
    The heart of a star!
Come love me forever
    As I chant this rune,
No one may dissever
    Us under the moon!

I rage and I stutter,
    Yet bow to thee here;
Each word you may utter
    Is meant for my ear.
My love is like silver
    And never a sin,
Although I may quiver
    Like some violin.

Come bring me a potion
    Of love most benign;
I'll drink me an ocean
    Of love like rare wine!
Now come to me lover
    Here coyly or bold,
For there is no other
    But thee who is gold!

The Sea King's Daughter

Down deep in this water
    She's conjured from silt:
The sea king's pale daughter
    From sea shells is built.

She's lovely as gold is;
    She rises in air.
Her gaze now so cold is,
    And scarlet her hair.

She walks on the seaside,
    Up out of the tide;
And stalks to the leeside,
    Her father's great pride.

She's pretty as dawn is,
    Most supple and fair;
Glorious, long is
    Her wet scarlet hair.

She dreams of a castle
    Perched high on this bluff;
A handsome young vassal
    For her is enough.

She coos to Orion
    The star of her birth,
For she is the scion
    Of Heaven and Earth.

It's only in dreams now
    She comes to this shore,
And everything seems now
    As it did before.

She once was a wife then,
    Both loved and adored,
A splendid sweet life then
    With her stalwart lord.

Now so like a dream is
    What went long before,
Just mist and all steam is
    That time from of yore.

Her lover she'll hail him
    This eve with a tune;
She swears she'll not fail him
    Here under the moon.

Oh, love that was altered,
    And harshly removed!
Oh, life that was haltered,
    And harshly reproved!

Down deep in this water
    She's conjured from silt:
The sea king's pale daughter
    From sea shells is built.

Arcanum

I dreamed of my darling down dales by the seaside,
Over opaline oceans and onion-domed fanes.
The two of us there in the bay on the leeside
Dreaming of green fields and warm summer rains.

We will ride the raw rivers in regions of sighing
On the banks of that stream under elm trees grown old,
And sail on our boat with the cool wind vying
With its decks polished teak and its railings of gold.

We'll sail on the currents hurrying, scurrying.
There watch how the sun sets in lavender skies,
As we stand at the wheel with the river murmuring;
We'll stare at each other with stars in our eyes.

I dreamed of my darling down dales by the seaside,
Over opaline oceans and onion-domed fanes.
The two of us there in the bay on the leeside
Dreaming of green fields and warm summer rains.

Vengeance for Io

I dreamt I was a Viking in a raid
Who plundered towns along this ancient coast,
And in one raid that I remember most
I took sweet Io, who was sore afraid.

Yet I was spellbound with her yard-long braid
Of magic red. Her flesh seemed like a ghost,
So pure and white, I drank to her a toast,
Then taunted her most lewdly as she prayed.

Yet I was cruel and ravished her withal,
And did such things as only demons do.
Her father followed after in the night
And stormed our stockade's meager wooden wall.
In his eyes I marked where murders brew—
We fought an hour there—he ran me through!

The Legs of Leviathan Loop

The legs of Leviathan loop through this sea
    As these tides will now monstrously rise.
These crows that are settled far out on the lea
Are now stricken with terror and rapidly flee
    Into these cold starry skies.

This listless Leviathan stirs up the silt
    And scatters the cod in a trice.
The headland's tall cliffs are all shattered, they tilt,
As the light from the moon like cold silver is spilt
    And covers this shore as would ice.

The foam from these breakers now bashes the beach
    While the spume is a pale salty mist.
These loons winging by now most loudly will screech;

The sea-wall itself has a long narrow breach
    That the mouth of Leviathan has kissed!

Nine Sirens twice lovely lie deep in their cave,
    And each one there sleeps like a child.
Immortally old, so they fear not the grave;
They heed not the kraken, though each is his slave,
    So they fear not when he runs wild.

The bones of a wizard, swept up with the tide,
    Reside now where flotsam's congealed.
His bones now have mixed with a merchant's young bride,
And their spirits this eve for one night will abide
    As they weather this outré ordeal!

These harried young harpies are frightened and pale
    In their nests on this cliff by the shore.
They shake and they tremble, turned white as a sail,
Where the force of the wind now blows in like a gale,
    So they take off and fly to the moor.

The goblins who haunt this steel ship in the sand
    That is covered with decades of rust,
They stare out in awe at the force of command
That this kraken now wields against sea, against land,
    And they fear such Leviathan lust!

Here gray spirits of ships once struck on this reef
    Will rise in this green moiling tea.
Death long ago culled them—a treacherous thief—
Who came in the night with a boatload of grief
    And drowned them all there in the sea.

The mermaids awake in their cave near the bay
    And cuddle their young ones in fear.
They know Leviathan, yet not his display
Of rancor and terror that causes dismay,
    And they think that their own deaths are near.

And then the sea calms, the waters recede,
    And the tide goes out in a rush!
It seems that Leviathan's sated his need,
As the moon's silver light here continues to bleed;
    The kraken falls back in a hush.

Fugue

Drown me in seas made tranquil
    Under ill-omened skies,
For I am now most thankful
    To be rid of all lies.
Let me grow glad in the knowing
    There where the silt seas blend,
There with the ghost winds blowing,
    When life's at an end.
Let me come up in the seasons
    Where gray ghosts thrive;
Leave me to mull on strange treasons
    That keep Sirens alive,
And leave me content with their reasons,
    Like bees in the hive.

I will sink once more with a notion
    Under these waves,
And I'll cull the cold ghosts from this ocean
    Right out of their graves;
I'll ring out old lovers at random,
    Beat these waves with a rod,
Line up my lovers in tandem
    Before the sea god.

The Flying Dutchman

I stood my watch hard by the great ship's wheel
And watched Orion rise up from the sea
To take its place and carefully watch me;
I felt the ship then shudder bow to keel!
Then saw a wan white sail that made me feel
Most odd, a ghost ship there, assuredly.
I'd heard the tales, and knew I could not flee—
The Dutchman rode the waves! Lord, she was real!

I turned her hard aport to seek escape,
Yet she came, flying, flying, through the seas!
I felt the very chill of death was in the air;
I thought that with some luck we'd make the Cape.
The Dutchman flew the faster on the breeze,
And when I looked once more, she was not there.

Flight 19*

We took off in December of that year.
Fort Lauderdale we'd never see again,
And now at dusk we are such ghostly men,
Who moan at night and shed a ghostly tear,
Still wearing flying boots and scarves and gear.
They searched the sea, the shore, the inland fen,
Yet we were lost beyond all human ken,
With nothing found but for the moon's cold leer.

Our old Avengers rest deep in the brine,
And while our flight is most outré, renowned,
Old pilots that get drunk on beer or wine,
Still shudder when they think how we were drowned.
And at the end when all the words are said
This haunted sea will not give up its dead.

*On December 5, 1945, five "Avenger" Grumman Torpedo Bombers took off from an airfield at the U.S. Naval Air Station, Fort Lauderdale, Florida, for a training flight and never returned. The weather that day was clear with some showers. The subsequent air-sea search and rescue is still the largest such rescue attempt ever undertaken. Yet absolutely nothing of Flight 19 was ever, or has ever been, found. They simply disappeared without a trace.

The Merman Tempts a Girl

Little girl in the amber shade
With steel-gray eyes so unafraid,
Come, little girl, come close to me,
Hard by this haunted, wine-dark sea.
I'll wind your hair in a pretty braid
Where mermaids bask in the silver shade,
Where foam ships ply at night or noon
 Set their sails to an opal moon.

Again and again you'll hear my plea,
Hard by this haunted, wine-dark sea.
Come right now, little girl, be bold,
And let me braid your hair of gold.
I'll take you under the ocean's dome
Way down deep to my hidden home,
Where mermaids love me dusk till dawn,
Over the seaweed's verdant lawn.

Let me place on your tawny neck
Torques of bronze from this old Greek wreck,
Jewel your fingers and jewel your toes,
With opals white as Arctic snows,
Above your hips a golden chain,
Gold of a lovely chatelaine.
I'll show you jewels of unusual size,
 And mirrors where peek your steel-gray eyes.

Never again see human leers,
As I jewel you with seashells on your ears
I'll tattoo kraken over your thighs
And show you where sunken treasure lies,
Whisper you love poems night and day
On this shore and across the bay;
I'm asking you now to be my wife,
Under the ocean all your life.

Ivory bracelets, polished bones,
Necklaces of green gemstones.
Against your legs the finest silk,
With trailing scarves as white as milk,
We'll dance along on the white-capped waves
Above the sunken old pirate graves.
All of this I will give to thee
If you would deign to marry me.

Lovesick

Lovesick love maketh me,
And where may I go?
Him who made the sea,
Yes, yes, He would know?
All day long I tarry,
My heart is astir.
Might I ask her to marry,
Yes, marry her?

Lovesick love maketh me,
Now where may I go?
Drown deep in this sea,
In the undertow?

Call of the Restless Sea

This restless sea yet calls me with the tide.
I hear its pounding waves so like a plea,
And that stupendous surf eternally
Sounds in my head and heart where I abide.
Her call is as some lover who has tried
To lure her fickle love back stealthily;
And, true enough, my heart yearns for the sea,
So at the moon I stand here now, seaside.

She reaches out with arms in foaming waves,
Her breath is salty as her heart is pure.
I know her touch, and know how well she laves
My body on this lonely midnight shore.
My heart is like a storm. I feel it stir!
I sigh and smile, for I will go to her!

I Wander

I wandered in the meadow,
I wandered in the lea,
A light and airy feather,

I blushed to see the sea.
And round the granite towers
That rise up to the clouds,
I moved through yellow flowers
Where shadows fell like shrouds.
Above these sandy beaches
I called out to the tides;
My lonely echo reaches
A thousand widowed brides.
I wandered in the meadow
Until the twilight fell
Upon this coast and headland
Down to the haunted dell.
This night became a dead land,
Yet why, I cannot tell. . . .

Sea Dream

These idols stand in a haunted land
    Wherein wan ghosts go sailing.
This storm's hard brand rolls up this sand,
    With banshees ever wailing.
I take my clue from an alien hue
    That's mixed with the twilight ever,
As I step unto her girlish coo,
    To that Siren sad and clever.

She's tall and wan, and as bright as the dawn;
    Her figure's fair and holy.

The fear is gone as I watch her don
    The sea spume, and this only!
Under these skies each spirit flies
    While trooping merrily,
And my Siren sighs as her grave blue eyes
    Peruse me warily!

And what should I think, upon the brink,
    When young love sweetly calls me,
Until I should sink without love's link,
    For it desperately now thralls me?
I breathe in the air while she is there,
    As her beauty is most stunning!
I would be wed, and our marriage bed
    Would be warm with her sweet cunning!

Now I cannot move, till her love will prove
    The anodyne to my aching.
She's filled some groove with kisses smooth
    Until I am left here shaking!
Now the moon's odd gleam, with its silver beam,
    Has left me lonely, sighing!
Like the sea foam's cream, it is all a dream,
    And I think now I am dying.

These idols stand in a haunted land
    Wherein wan ghosts go sailing.
This storm's hard brand rolls up this sand,
    With banshees ever wailing.

I take my clue from an alien hue
    That's mixed with the twilight ever,
As I step unto her girlish coo,
    To that Siren sad and clever.

Merlin's Daughter

I dreamt of a deep and splendid pool
    With dark and icy water.
Ah, up, up she rose now bare and cool,
    And all men there besought her.
Quite tall and slim and no man's fool,
    For some sorceress had taught her,
That beauty and magic will ever rule,
    And they call her Merlin's daughter.
She came to me, and I may not tell
    How she dripped with that crystal water.
How her eyes were huge, and cast a spell
    As my muscles then grew tauter.
Now all my soul would sigh and yell,
    Where the moon's light there had brought her.
My heart she enslaved, there on the fell,
    As in my arms I caught her!
And all of her sighs would sting, impel
    My soul for that girl from the water.
And true enough, my soul I would sell,
    To cherish Fay Merlin's daughter.

Her kisses twice sweet, and could compel.
    A harlot? No, though be sure enough I bought her.
I gave up my heart, I gave up my soul,
    Right there where all men besought her.
And, in effect, she swallowed me whole,
    Did she, right here by the water.

Veronique

My love had wings to tarry
    On seaside and the sea,
Where West winds fought to carry
    My lover back to me.
Dark tides went raging, sweeping
    These sands eternally,
My tears like rain went weeping
    For life and love of thee.

These headlands hold my yearnings,
    For life and love and more,
As storm winds in their turnings
    Rake all this haunted shore.
Yet still you come not after
    The sea has grown morose,
And gone's your gentle laughter,
    My precious, fickle rose.

My flighty little linnet,
>   So proud and sure and fleet,
Eschewed the ring and spinet.
>   Thy lips, my love, were sweet!
Your flesh a lovely umber,
>   For all your men and me,
Your lovers without number,
>   Hard by this haunted sea.

My love had wings to borrow
>   The flight of eagles high,
Yet now there's only sorrow,
>   I'm driven from that sky.
And still those tides go sweeping
>   The shoals and shore and sand,
And yet the sky is weeping
>   Upon this dismal land.

A Sea Change

My love for her has come to naught,
>   I've wasted precious Time.
A low-born girl will now be sought,
>   Out in some far-off clime.

I'll seek her there in old Shanghai,
>   In brothels dark and drear,
Or seek her there in far Mumbai,
>   In slums and bring her here.

Down alleyways long lost to sin
    I'll seek my dark-eyed girl,
A stoic drudge who's dull and thin,
    Most dark and no pale pearl.

I found that Hindi woman then
    Who claimed she was nineteen,
Who said she knew a thousand men,
    To leave that place was keen.

I bought her for the merest song
    And sailed away at dusk.
I washed her down before we'd gone
    And scented her with musk.

Once on the sea she seemed to change,
    More beautiful and tall,
And in her dark eyes something strange
    Made them exceptional!

Her voice's timbre changed as well:
    It was no longer loud;
Her voice became a sweet soft bell,
    Her aspect now seemed proud.

And she bewitched me on that ship,
    Her dark hair like a cloak;
The brass ring in her pretty lip,
    It made me gulp and choke.

I fell afraid of her at sea,
    At her intense façade.
Before we docked I set her free,
    Her bearing like some god!

A Sea Spell in Winter

Spells hung upon the winter breeze,
Blown in from the Hebrides
Like icy blades they cut and stung;
Upon the winter breeze spells hung.

These crested waves they billowed there
Above them frigid winter air;
Below them sleep both kings and knaves—
They billowed there these crested waves.

Here in the sand they're buried deep,
This ship where ruined sailors sleep;
All of her crew, each able hand,
They're buried deep here in the sand.

This midnight tide, it hurries in,
The air's grown icy, cold and thin;
This hulking wreck, its shattered side,
It hurries in this midnight tide.

These long years gone she came to rest,
Within this bay's white sandy breast;
Here spirits walk until the dawn,
She came to rest these long years gone.

Lure of the Siren

Under these stars that fade and droop,
    The bay is bathed in a silver loop.
Up from the shore where great tides fan
    Is a new reed chair of brown rattan.
A Siren bends at the waist to stoop,
    To laugh in the face of a drowning man—
One of many an age-old troop
    Lured by lust to an ultimate grief,
Drowned at dawn on the coral reef.

She sits down on her brown reed chair,
    Inhales the cool electric air,
Sighs that there's no more men to lure
    To the reef to drown on her lonely shore;
As she combs her long and ebon hair
    Dreams of the wreck the night before,
While over the sea her dark eyes stare,
    Sighs once more and dreams of the deep,
Basks in the sun in her Siren sleep.

Lovers, Ghosts, and Monsters

Vengeance

My love's separation, despair, each a goad,
    These bind me and drive with a will!
Now with a vengeance I travel that road
To slay all her suitors who sow or have sowed
    The seeds of my lusting to kill!

She left me one dusk for a mere beggar's boy;
    They left in a barque from the bay.
I tracked them for weeks, all my skills would employ;
She left him one night as a mere useless toy—
    With cold steel I then made him pay.

I tracked her through fens and a dangerous moor,
    Fought werewolves, a giant, a witch.
At dusk I would bellow for my paramour,
And my voice it would echo from hillside to shore;
    My hatred developed a twitch.

I strode through the towns and each village alone,
    And Lord, they were fearful of me!
They knew me as fearsome, a heart made of stone,
In terror showed kindness, now that much I'll own.
    Then they told me she'd taken to sea.

I bought me a schooner and hired nine tars,
    Each a cutthroat down to his bones.
They said she went west, so we charted the stars;

I slept well that night, dreamt of cold avatars,
    Who set me on gold-plated thrones.

My lover had taken a merchant in tow,
    And they sailed on his high-masted ship;
And avid was I for a strong wind to blow,
That I might catch them both and swift death there bestow—
    Revenge tastes most sweet when you sip!

That blow came along like some almighty hand
    And battered us there like a toy;
It crushed our ship there and ground us to sand,
And washed up our bodies on some foreign strand,
    And all of my hates would destroy.

And now in the night I will soar on the sea,
    Or glide past these headlands afar.
I've lost all that rancor that once consumed me,
My twisted old bones bleach seaside alee,
    And shine in the moon like a star.

My love's separation, despair, each a goad,
    These bind me and drive with a will!
Now with a vengeance I travel that road
To slay all her suitors who sow or have sowed
    The seeds of my lusting to kill!

Death on the Moor

I have seen the wounded terror
That haunts the midnight vale—
A thing of sin and error
That answers not my hail.

It moves within the bracken;
It trundles down the moor;
Its pace it will not slacken—
I'm frightened to my core!

It is sleek with salty evil;
Its steps both light and cold,
A thing remote, medieval—
By evil it's controlled.

Now it slinks across the bridges,
And it tarries cross the moor,
Down below the shadowed ridges
Where frightened birds there soar.

It lures me! I can scent it,
Its strong and sweet aloes,
And its magic, beauty lent it!
Ah, now I know it knows!

For I know that it's twice lonely,
Shaped like a comely girl.
This eve it wants me only
To feel its flesh of pearl!

Her silhouette is handsome:
She's pretty and not coy.
My soul soon none may ransom;
She calls me "pretty boy!"

She's lovely and a beauty,
She rises from the fen;
I feel now it's my duty
Of all of living men

To grasp her and to hold her,
Then crush her in my arms;
To kiss her, then to fold her,
To know her monstrous charms.

Now like some glass she dashes
Me to the peat and sod;
She rips me and she thrashes
Me with an iron rod!

I am broken and I'm bleeding;
Over me she towers,
A fool who's never heeding,
She kills and then devours!

Stars That Sunder

Cold are these stars that sunder
    Their foeman too soon;
So loud these hooves that thunder
    Here under the moon.

Sweet this Siren who's calling,
    Most sweet and fair,
Quite mad the one she's enthralling
    With her yellow hair.

Gray is the moonlight dashing
    Upon these blue stones,
And high are these combers crashing
    Over drowned bones;
And shy is this mermaid humming
    A lover's tune;
Breathless her lover's coming
    Under the moon.

The Wizard Makes a Girl

I conjured love from thinnest of thin air
And called her Arabella, on that day.
Agile, wicked lovely, was made for play,
And red as new-spilled blood her long, long hair.
Athletic she, and graceful, sleek and spare,
My slightest wish she'd eagerly obey;
I dressed her in fine silks from Mandalay,
And jewels exquisite and exceeding rare.

And then one night there was a subtle change;
Her smile was less impressive than before,
And something changed with how she hugged and kissed.
I rose at dawn, alone, gazed on the grange;

There with a boy I saw her on the moor.
I wept for love. She will be sorely missed.

The Lover

Love is left by this cold dark river,
    Cold and dead in the gathered dusk.
Love's deep hurt makes the sad soul shiver;
    All that's left is the scent of musk,
As she is gone where none may find her:
Only the risen spirits mind her.
No love in life would ever bind her
    Beneath this harsh moon's icy tusk.

Thin is my shadow under heaven,
    There where the ghosts in darkness cling.
Their number seventy times seven,
    Where love recalled retains its sting.
I move alone to brood and ponder
Over these leas where werewolves wander,
Over the fen and moorland yonder,
    Until the abbey's dawn bells ring.

I coil with the winds that swirl and hasten,
    There by the sunken garden's pool;
This crisp cold air will clear and chasten,
    Yet ever the cold is biting, cruel.
Swift was the love I learned to master,
Love was a game, and I played faster,

Dream Lover

Hidden therein was death, disaster.
    My lover grew exceeding cool.

Soft is this breeze that gently calls me,
    Haunts this garden in June and May.
Harsh is her gaze that gently thralls me,
    Here each dusk where the frail ghosts play.
Now in the dark I wander duly,
My lover sits near the roses coolly;
As ever she smiles both stern and cruelly
    To stare beyond this haunted bay.

Love is left by this cold dark river,
    Cold and dead in the gathered dusk;
Love's deep hurt makes the sad soul shiver,
    All that's left is the scent of musk,
As she is gone where none may find her:
Only the risen spirits mind her.
No love in life would ever bind her
    Beneath this harsh moon's icy tusk.

Idol Found in the Woods

I found a shattered idol in the wood,
Hung with ivy, one mile up from the shore,
Its eyes and face of bone and similor;
Huge conifers hung near it like a hood.
Perhaps eight thousand years alone it stood,
Shaped from some unknown rock, some star-borne ore,

Its likeness to some mythic carnivore,
About this stone was sure the scent of blood!

I backed away, ran headlong down the trail,
And thought I heard it stand, begin to move,
And then I heard a grim titanic wail!
Now if it came to life, I could not prove,
But reached the shore that empties in the bay,
Dove in, and swam so far, so far away.

The Constant Lover

Atop this purple palisade
A tower's gleaming in the mist,
So like a column deftly made
Of gem-cut purple amethyst.

These clouds at dusk begin to fade
As dim stars spread their vast festoon,
While shapes move in the tower's shade
Below this lamp-like hunter's moon.

Here one frail ghost who is so keen
To climb this stone-cut ashy stair
This graceful girl tonight is seen,
As pale as chalk with flowing hair.

She calls across the far arcade;
She hopes that he will come now soon,

Her young lieutenant's long delayed,
She sighs for her long-dead dragoon.

She thinks, perhaps, his ship will dock
Below this tower on the coast;
Against the quay, hard by the rock,
She knows not that they're each a ghost.

Atop this purple palisade
A tower's gleaming in the mist,
So like a column deftly made
Of gem-cut purple amethyst.

I Ride the Nightmare

Through dreams I ever seek her,
Though I grow faint and weaker,
My prospects seem but bleaker,
    Deep in nightmarish sleep.
I plumb such dark abysses,
Yet each probe fails and misses,
I seek her dream-wrought kisses,
    My way's both dark and steep.

And yet I'm filled with wonder,
Within my dark dreams' thunder,
With some dreams pulled asunder,
    By things so dark, unknown.

So long I've sought to hold her,
Love her, bless her scold her,
And in my arms I'd fold her,
    Yet I am still alone!

Come out, my green-eyed lover,
From dreams that none discover,
And over you I'll hover,
    Like desert jinn you own.
My sleep is spent in crying,
While brooding, searching, trying,
Can you not see I'm dying?
    My face now pale as bone.

My nightmares make me quiver,
I sweat with fear and shiver,
From these I would deliver
    My lover to my side.
These dreams turn musty, moldy,
Their breezes sting me coldly,
And yet I go on boldly,
    And still the nightmare ride!

Through dreams I ever seek her,
Though I grow faint and weaker,
My prospects seem but bleaker,
    Deep in nightmarish sleep.
I plumb such dark abysses,
Yet each probe fails and misses,
I seek her dream-wrought kisses,
    My way's both dark and steep.

The Fell at Twilight

I walk the fell at twilight
In winter and in fall,
Where moonglow throws a highlight
Against the garden wall.
The oaks tinged with burnt umber,
As plodding shadows lumber,
And all the world's in slumber,
With silence over all.

This lake like flat black glass is
So like a jet-black jewel
As movement in the grass is
Sea winds that roil the pool.
Here by its shores is weeping,
A girl no longer sleeping,
Whose memory is reaping
A past twice mean and cruel.

She dreams of summer gardens,
Yet winter's close at hand.
She'll weep as this pool hardens
When cold air stalks the land.
Her soldier-lover's lying
In fields with sad ghosts sighing,
And so it is she's crying
Warm tears that wet the sand.

She sighs once more and wonders,
Beside her lonely pool,
Why wars exist, or thunders;
Both seem so awful, cruel.
I watch her all day tarry;
She seems too wan and airy,
A ghost or childlike fairy,
A lovely little jewel.

I walk the fell at twilight,
In winter and in fall,
Where moonglow throws a highlight
Against the garden wall.
The oaks tinged with burnt umber,
As plodding shadows lumber,
And all the world's in slumber,
With silence over all.

A Midnight Tryst

These tides break boldly—I will go
To fetch my lover drowned alone
Upon a night so long ago;
I mark her throaty, ghostly groan.

Now come, my darling, from the deep
Up out of Time and out of Space,
And reawaken from your sleep
And let me see your Siren's face.

Cast off the chill of centuries;
Stand once more so statuesque.
I hear your whisper on the breeze,
The risen moon's an arabesque.

Cast off the salt, cast off the spume!
Your body's like to polished brass.
I sense your rare and strong perfume,
I watch you through these combers pass.

Once more your hair is long and black,
No more a ghost, a fragile shade.
Your sweeping hair glides down your back,
A river in a dark cascade!

I hear the ocean's murmuring;
You stand there now, yet still a shade.
I watch your body shimmering,
And like a ghost you fade and fade!

These tides break boldly—I will go
To fetch my lover drowned alone,
Upon a night so long ago;
I mark her throaty, ghostly groan.

Wizard Love

She is both cruel and kinder,
    Her eyes like satin seas;
Yet I can read the star-streams
Whose fickle whims may mar dreams,

And seek her out and find her
    As leaves will find a breeze.
She is both cruel and kinder,
    Her eyes like satin seas.

My magics will so wall her,
    Though all the stars rebel.
She sometimes seems a fairy,
When laughing, coy and airy;
She comes not when I call her,
    But casts her elfin spell!
My magics will so wall her,
    Though all the stars rebel.

One May our lovely garden
    Went gray and dead at noon,
To fill me with a sorrow,
With no joy left to borrow,
While my poor heart would harden
    Beneath the icy moon!
One May our lovely garden
    Went gray and dead at noon.

And with all went my lover
    Beyond the bourn of life.
Each day, though I am clever,
Goes on it seems forever,
As no joy I discover
    As she is gone, my wife.
And with it went my lover,
    Beyond the bourn of life.

The Necromancer

My magics now will mend her,
My long-dead lover, slender,
Whose kisses were twice tender
    When she and I would meet.
A guileless girl, no schemer,
Sweet charmer and a dreamer,
All men would ever deem her
    The sweetest of the sweet.

Fell ill in mid-September,
She died in late December,
And too well I remember
    My sorrow knew no bounds.
And while my heart was burning,
My soul in turmoil churning,
My lust was always yearning
    To see her on these grounds.

I curse the gods and heavens,
No love my anger leavens,
I curse my luck by sevens,
    There in my deep despair.
Then at the witching hour,
I know with magic power
That she once more would flower—
    Once more I'd kiss her hair!

I'd call my supple dancer,
I'd make black Death then answer,
I'd be that necromancer
    To call her from the tomb!
I conjured her one twilight,
The moon shone down a highlight;
There through my chamber's skylight
    I called her back from doom.

Now from those shadows falling
No voice came forth in calling,
It seemed the night was stalling,
    I failed to hear her there.
I found myself then sighing,
And bitterly was crying,
And in that darkness dying,
    Fast dying of despair.

In Amber

Far from Triassic forests, in the glare
Of that gigantic sun that warmed strange seas,
And continents of vast immensities,
Trees rose two hundred feet into the air.
Huge conifers almost beyond compare,
Their amber saps trapped ants and flies and fleas,
Mosquitoes, spiders, and odd honeybees,
And caught these ancient insects unaware.

* * *

Is not our love, my dear, like such as these—
A pretty piece of jewelry in the hand,
Like some porcelain from the Japanese,
A kiln-dried urn they polished in the sand?
So very pretty and full of allure,
Our amber love dead as the dinosaur.

The Abandoned Lover

Over ever
Is our love,
Clever sever
All thereof.
Heighten, frighten
What was ours.
Never brighten,
Deadly stars!

Fatal lover,
Fatal mate,
Under, over,
Insensate!
Baited, sated,
Till the dawn,
You were fated
To be gone!

Tall and pretty,
Sly and sleek,
Cool and witty,
Shy and meek.
Dripping scarlet,
Splendid gowns,
Scheming harlot
For your clowns!

Lips of sweetness,
Huge eyes green,
Lovely neatness,
Guileful, mean!
Cunning lover,
Ardent, fierce,
My love smother,
My heart pierce!

Pale, reliant,
Wooing girl,
Moody, silent,
Pretty pearl!
Love and like me,
As a wife,
Yet you strike me
With love's knife!

Crafty eyeful,
Meek and mild,
Sly and guileful,

Wicked child!
Cruel and crueler.
Moon or sun,
Heartless ruler,
Evil one!

Frail and royal,
Bright, severe;
Never loyal
Dark and drear!
How you made me
With your art,
Then betrayed me,
Stole my heart.

Dark Machinations

These dark machinations of marked mantic spells
    Are woven by one who is fay.
She's soft and astute and serene and she sells
Darkest dark magic that ignites and impels:
    This sorceress lives by the bay.

She's tall and most taut and a talented girl,
    It seems she is merely a child.
She's old as the moon! Could seduce any earl,
A temptress whose power she'll furl or unfurl;
    Sedate yet can quickly turn wild.

Her hair is perfumed and is long as the Nile,
    A sly and most sensuous tart.
Exotic her eyes, yet they harbor such bile,
Such power she has to bewitch and beguile,
    Can break a man's hard granite heart.

She seems but pure grace and is wan as the moon,
    And her anger a thing that can slay.
She can rage like the wind of the darkest typhoon,
She's part made of lightning and never jejune,
    In her castle hard by this bay.

I met her one night on this coast in a storm,
    Alone on that high headland there.
She spoke not a word, was receptive and warm;
In a tight-fitting gown her incredible form
    Was crowned by her long luscious hair.

We spoke of the sea and its cold fickle tides,
    The whiteness of tide-driven foam,
And marked how each wave with the cliff face collides.
The pale soaring comets she told me were brides
    Of avatars heading for home.

She told me of realms that were foreign and cruel,
    Of strange sorcery and of art.
Surprised that she told me that she felt a fool,
Was bored with her power and absolute rule,
    That loneliness pierced her poor heart.

I dreaded her talk as I dreaded her near,
    For fickle she was and most dark.
I trembled there so, a full victim of fear,
The moon in her eye caught one small crystal tear,
    There under the sky's starry arc.

She touched my hand softly but then turned away,
    And back to her castle she strolled.
The moonlight fell oddly right there on the bay;
Its halo of silver in strangest array
    Was limned in a sorcerous gold.

These dark machinations of marked mantic spells
    Are woven by one who is fay.
She's soft and astute and serene and she sells
Darkest dark magic that ignites and impels:
    This sorceress lives by the bay.

Rolling the Bones

I rolled the bones as the whispered moans
    Of ghosts moved on the fell,
As out of the fen nine ghostly men
    Rose from the seventh hell.

They cursed me there in the upper air
    As I rolled the dice again,
Yet the night was gray and I lost my way
    And the dice rolled in the fen.

I stood and I strode to the old shore road,
    And I mumbled a single spell;
Then a girl named Eve would tug at my sleeve,
    And she ran with me pell-mell.

Then down that road to an old abode
    She pulled me through the door;
Then she kissed my lips and pulled my hips,
    And she whispered: "Paramour!"

Now I can't recall what befell me withal
    On that eve with my own dark Eve:
At dawn I'd stare at that red stain there
    Of her lipstick on my sleeve!

Tan Girl

Under this bridge's granite span,
Under this werewolf moon that glows,
A lovely girl both limber, tan
Haunts these ruined old châteaux.

Her hair, quite long, is velvet black;
She's willowy and razor thin.
Her hair a cloak down her bare back,
Against her soft and nymph-like skin.

Her fine lips whisper in a prayer;
The midnight winds are strong with sighs,
While cool as ice the autumn air,
Two deep black pools her shining eyes.

One pretty hand she moves to sweep
The glory of her ebon locks;
Her curving hips both smooth and steep,
Her impish, elfin head she cocks.

And magic drips from her like dew
From fruit trees in lost Paradise:
A girl that only kings might woo,
She is that pearl of greatest price.

She places then each pretty hand
Upon her gently curving hips;
She seems like one known to command—
A lone tear down her tanned cheek slips.

Under this bridge's granite span,
Under this werewolf moon that glows,
A lovely girl both limber, tan
Marks the ghosts on far plateaus.

She-Wolf

Tall, pale and sleek, with sandal straps of red,
Her hair of gushing gold tossed thick and free.
I followed her through forests patiently,
Up to a beetling cliff face overhead.
Into a cave she walked and made her bed—
Sweet hay and grass. I watched this entity

Sprawl at full length, while smiling pleasantly:
Such pristine beauty took away my dread.

I stood and watched that regal girl transform
Into a she-wolf with a coat of gray.
Her blue eyes fluttered, raging like a storm.
Those feral eyes filled me with such dismay,
I fled that cave and ran back down the trail,
And ever hear that preternatural wail!

Night of the Banshee

Peal upon peal from this echoing arbor,
    And walled with old oaks on this hill,
The banshee cries out with an infinite ardor,
Then circles this fen the lea and the harbor,
    Here in this deep winter's chill.

She screams for her lover once lost and then taken
    By waves in a giant typhoon;
And the sound of her screams these rafters have shaken,
This wandering banshee forever forsaken—
    Like a wolf she howls at the moon.

I was down in that arbor one winter alone
    And saw there a weeping young girl:
She was slight and pathetic, mere skin and bone;
She would wring her small hands and exhale a soft moan,
    Like a banner her hair would unfurl.

She pleaded with me and she asked me for aid;
    I sat there and touched one small hand.
She was so deathly cold, like to ice was she made,
Yet she spoke in soft words like some smooth serenade,
    Which made me then feel rather grand.

Her eyes were like oceans that know constant storm,
    Her wan lips were made to beguile;
She admitted the cold and she wished to be warm,
She asked me to keep her, protect her from harm;
    Her lips nearly curved in a smile.

And then she rose up like a cobra in rage,
    Her hair turned a scraggily white;
Her face then collapsed in a hideous phage,
And her howling nothing might staunch or assuage—
    Then she flew off into the night!

My door is twice bolted in winter for fear,
    And I keep an old flintlock nearby.
I sit by my sill and I see her appear,
And I shake as I watch as that banshee comes near,
    And I cringe to hear her loud cry!

Peal upon peal from this echoing arbor,
    And walled with old oaks on this hill,
The banshee cries out with an infinite ardor,
Then circles this fen the lea and the harbor,
    Here in this deep winter's chill.

She Soared Upon the Wind

She soared upon the wind, a bird of prey;
Her wings became slim arms when on the ground.
Her talons now were feet securely bound
In sandals with silk straps of blue and gray.
And when she walked her hips would slyly sway,
Yet she could move without the slightest sound;
With hair like flaming gold her head was crowned;
She churned men's hearts to roiling disarray.

I boldly sought her out there in the dusk
And took her gently by her red-nailed hand,
And as I did I turned an empty husk:
I tried to speak, my tongue went dry as sand.
Her eyes, like lances, pierced my heart, she smiled.
She knew that I then, too, was now beguiled.

Illicit Rendezvous

It's night on the heather
    And far from the shore;
The moonlight will measure
    This long trail of spoor.
This stern beast is avid,
    And avid for blood,
Most wild and twice rabid—
    Leaves tracks in the mud.

The werewolf is stalking
    Behind and before;
Soft whispers and talking
    From ghosts by the door.
Illicit and smugly,
    Dark Eva arrives,
Twice petulant, ugly,
    She always connives.

A lamia lonely,
    She changes her form;
Can turn pretty only
    By her pendant charm
That hangs at her bodice
    Of leprous white:
It turns her a goddess
    For all the dark night!

We meet each December
    Ere comes the typhoon,
Or June and September
    Here under the moon;
We kiss and we wrestle
    Here under this sky,
We snuggle and nestle,
    Yet know it's a lie!

It's night on the heather
    And far from the shore,
The moonlight will measure
    This long trail of spoor.

This stern beast is avid,
    And avid for blood,
Most wild and twice rabid—
    Leaves tracks in the mud.

The Madness of the Moon

The madness of the moon has made me yearn
For things bizarre and things beyond outré.
Too long I've tarried in this moonstruck bay
Until what's real I can no more discern.
A Siren sought me, yet her love I'd spurn;
Instead, through arcane lore I'd find my way,
And carnal temptings I would then defray,
But in the end with rabid lust I'd burn!

So on this night I seek her at the tide:
Cassandra is her name and thus I call,
Until my echoes with tall cliffs elide.
I burn for her and long to be her thrall,
Yet she is cruel and slyly waits alone,
Until I quiver, weeping, pale as bone.

Withered Roses

Our love is no more holy:
    We've sued to other gods,
Together or each solely,
    We've beaten love with rods,

And taken all our kisses
>   That love once gladly bred,
Now turned to vipers' hisses,
>   And left them here for dead.

Entangled and entwining,
>   Our schemes all fell apart;
To hell we've left designing
>   The patterns of our heart.
No more we see the roses
>   That flowered in our eyes,
For hate each eye now closes,
>   Each flower withers, dies.

I drink my cup of sorrow,
>   I drink it to the lees;
There's no more joy to borrow,
>   Adrift on savage seas.
Ah, let me feel the dagger,
>   Long dulled or thick with rust,
For gone is all my swagger—
>   Give me that steel's death-thrust!

Now as my body quivers,
>   I dream of sweet aloes;
My blood flows out in rivers
>   As red as any rose.
I wonder if she's smiling,
>   I think I see her there,
Bewitching and beguiling,
>   With my last gasp for air.

Forlorn

I dream of long-rift valleys and the horn
That sounds from hidden grottos in the dells,
Chants from a slender sorceress whose spells
Have left me sorrowful and so forlorn.
A pretty girl who loves to so adorn
Her ears and throat with polished blue seashells,
And on her ankles wears such tiny bells,
Purloined by her beyond some haunted bourn.

She moves her hands most deftly in the dark
To conjure beings from some nether sphere,
And softly sings below that huge white ark,
The moon, until her star-born lover will appear.
And then she gazes gladly out to sea:
I'm tossed aside, she has grown bored with me.

Lycanthropy at Dusk

If lupine women sue me through the glade
At dusk when all the trees will bend and look,
I'd be awake in dreams by this cool brook
And dally with a nymph deep in the shade.
Her long and golden hair I would unbraid;
Her belt of crimson leather I'd unhook,
And kiss her throat and shoulder at the crook—
Yet of those werewolf women I'm afraid.

* * *

And then I heard their snarls and wolfish shouts;
I fled my nymph girl through the twisted oak,
To hide among the ruined stone redoubts.
Those lupine girls surrounded me like smoke.
"There is no chance!" I heard them howl and bray:
I know that soon this night they'll have their way.

Purchased Love

I took the green elixir that she gave
And drained the contents of that pewter cup:
That brothel girl smiled as I drank it up.
I dropped it then and smashed it on the pave.
My face and eyes with kisses she would lave,
And from her restless mouth would I then sup.
Her purchased love would all my heart disrupt.
I woke up in her bed as in a grave.

I fled that brothel by its dark rear door;
My mind spun wildly, shaken to the bone.
She had my heart through some most black glamour;
I knew I would return, and me she'd own,
Now such a slave, I'd give her all my gold,
And while my lust burned hot, hers would grow cold.

Fable

In dreams I measure
My girl, my treasure,
The queen of pleasure,
    The salve for pain.
This crown above her
In dreams discover,
I watch it hover,
    My love sustain.
Beauty and splendor
Her kiss can render,
So coy and slender,
    My precious jewel.
My love's entire,
My heart's desire,
Her love's pure fire
    Never grows cool.

In June and Maytime,
Nighttime and daytime,
Ever is playtime
    Under these stars.
Girl ever beaming,
Unearthly seeming,
Sets me to dreaming
    Far beyond Mars.
Her love now blesses
Me with caresses,

Her silken dresses
>   Glow like the moon.
Scarce am I able
To speak or stand stable,
She's but a fable,
>   Gone all too soon!

Under These Stars

Girl ever beaming,
Unearthly seeming,
Sets me to dreaming
>   Far beyond Mars.
Her love now blesses
Me with caresses,
Her silken dresses
>   Glow like the moon.
Scarce am I able
To speak or stand stable,
She's but a fable,
>   Gone all too soon!

Girl in the Dunes

Far over the midnight sand the dunes
So palely glow like stone baboons,
>   While out of the sand I see a girl
>   Spin lightly as her long skirts swirl.

The cool and whispered wind chants runes;
    She's pretty and she's pale as pearl.
The low hills lurk like dead dragoons;
    Laughing alone as the gray stars rise,
    I mark the mystery in her eyes.

One skip, one jump, and a little hop,
Before me now she'll stand and stop;
    And she coyly eyes me with a smile,
    I feel her girlish cunning, guile.
Then oddly to my knees I drop,
    She muses over me awhile,
Bends slow to kiss my head on top:
    Like silver I see her shining bright,
    Then turn and flee into the night!

She

Sway and swagger
    On the lawn,
Eyes a dagger
    Pierce the dawn.

Storms have rumbled
    In her eyes,
Red hair tumbled
    To her thighs.

Long legs curving,
    Hear her sigh,

So unnerving,
    I will die.

Keeps on coming,
    I'm afraid,
My heart's drumming,
    I'm unmade!

Keep your distance,
    Thou art fay,
My resistance
    Ebbs away.

Now she holds me
    In her arms,
Soothes and folds me
    With her charms.

The Black Comet

Under the eyes of night the web
Of far-off stars hangs in festoon,
And there beyond the dark domains
The stars will ebb,
While past the moon
The icy pains,
For love has flown.

My heart so like a hammered stone,
No lover's vigil I will keep.

Instead I'll walk like Death, alone,
Mere flesh and bone,
Lost in the deep.
I twist and moan,
For love has flown.

When twilight falls and shadows steal
Across these courtyards of despair,
I stalk the land devoid of sleep.
No salve may heal,
So thin this air.
No watch I keep,
For love has flown.

Now one black comet passes by:
I mark its path; it comes for me.
All stars align within this sky,
Eternity.
For such I sigh,
I faint, I die,
For love has flown.

Ghost Poet

These high-built walls and brickwork out of plumb,
Bright moonlight streams into this haunted hall:
Here sudden death would all my dreams forestall.
See now the silver ghost that I've become?
My bardic voice is silent, long since dumb.

I'm like the mist that floats across the mall,
Down to the ancient oak, a seneschal,
That will, too, in the end, like me succumb.

The wind comes up from off the nearby shore;
The midnight sky looms darkly, black as lead,
And rushing down the shattered corridor
The wind stirs up the bones of those long dead.
It seems the heavy winter breeze has thinned;
The dawn comes near, I vanish on the wind.

Regret

In winter when moon shadows cast
    Their lengths around this minaret,
Within this windswept snowy vast,
    I come to learn, anew, regret.

Its door is buried deep in drifts,
    Its granite walls now cracked and glazed,
And in the night my spirit lifts
    To once again be so amazed.

So long ago we two would meet,
    Below its crumbled parapet,
Yet now hard by the winding street
    I come to learn, anew, regret.

These vines are leafless as they climb;
    Your soft huge eyes were black as jet.

The old stones' surface caked with rime,
    Once more I learn, anew, regret.

I think I see you fringed in white
    Above the sill where sad stars set;
The wind howls coldly on this night
    When once again I learn regret.

I curse this place, this winter cold,
    The stars that limn this minaret
That makes these snowdrifts tinged with gold.
    This place where I have learned regret!

Oh, take me from this place, far, far,
    For now I see her silhouette
Before a huge and evil star,
    For now I learn, too well, regret.

Clarice

My candle burns here at the sill;
Its flame is ramrod straight and tall.
The humid night is dark and still,
Where shadows fall.

I think I hear a madrigal,
As my poor heart begins to break.
I think I hear Clarice's call
Upon the lake.

The old oak stands, a seneschal,
While in my grief I'd love to take
And drown my grief across the mall,
Deep in the lake.

I watch the moonlight's silver spill
Across that same witch-haunted mall,
And there it gives my soul a chill
Where shadows fall.

I thought I was invincible,
Yet nothing will my sadness slake;
My every tryst a bitter gall,
Hard by this lake.

Beyond the lake the grain fields sprawl;
No other lover will I take,
For all my lust is animal,
Here by this lake.

My candle burns here at the sill;
Its flame is ramrod straight and tall.
The humid night is dark and still,
Where shadows fall.

The Love Potion

The eye-of-newt I drop below
The surface of this magic brew;
This potion will such strength bestow,
This love spell that I now pursue.

A lock of dead man's hair will bind
These rare aloes and mystic spice
To charm the lover, make him blind,
Or melt her heart as cold as ice.

I mix them here so carefully;
One drop, a fickle harlot sin,
An urchin from the deepest sea,
Stirred with a secret scarlet sin.

A penny from a poor man's purse;
I watch this foaming flagon rise,
The power of a wizard's curse,
Mixed with cold tears from dragon's eyes.

I whisper words of woe and weal
And call dead spirits from the sea;
It thickens now, yet won't congeal—
This potion's done! It's brewed for thee!

The Princess of Grant Street

She said she was a princess from the coast,
Not from our world, but from the moons of Mars,
That she was kidnapped by cruel avatars,
But she escaped she said, and how she'd boast!
Full of herself, this girl, pale as a ghost.
Her eyes were brown and dull like dying stars,
She worked at night the Grant Street pubs and bars:
I bought her love one fleet hour as her host.

And afterwards she said she wanted tea.
I thought it odd, but brewed her some right there;
Half-dressed, she drank it with such majesty;
So regally she tossed her long red hair.
She looked so utterly alone, so small,
Her tale was strange, yet I believed it all!

The Spire and the Ghost

To the spire
She will climb—
Higher, higher
Out of Time.
Down the ages
Down the years,
Ancient sages
Vanished tears.

She shines whitely
There alone,
Only nightly,
Pale as bone;
Ghost girl soaring
To the sky,
Gray tides roaring
Just nearby.

In the darkness
She appears,

In such starkness
Through the years;
Ghostly whiteness
As she goes,
Glaring brightness
Like to snows.

All will eye her
As she climbs;
Ogle, spy her
At these times;
Come and mark her
As she moves,
Grim and starker,
Love she proves!

Warlocks and Mages

Warlocks and mages and castles entire,
Hard by this seaside where banyans suspire,
Nubile and breezy
Young nymphs of the wood,
Their beauty lifts me,
Well as it should.

Warlocks and mages with deep-seated schemes,
They people my visions and people my dreams,
Yet I seek lovers,
Wan Sirens sublime;

Shed their cloak covers—
They're scented with thyme.

Warlocks and mages—I've kept them at bay,
I'm done with their posturing, idle display!
It's nymphs I seek out,
Pale girls that I crave,
Their kisses I seek out,
Ere I rest in my grave.

Sower of Discord

In wild storms as they pester and pillage
    I glide on the grimmest black cloud;
As these winds destroy farmland and village,
    I hover there like a dark shroud,
And glide past the oaks and the river,
    Hammer hard on the old inn's weak door,
As its dwellers gasp and they shiver,
    I move on the moor.

I then haunt the fen and the castle
    And sweep through its courtyards of slate,
Till I rouse up the frightened old vassal
    And rattle his huge iron gate.
The shutters I'll pull from its towers
    To smash them on stable and wall,
And people will cringe at my powers
    In bedroom and hall.

It's only in winter with rancor
    That I'll ride like a ghost on the wind,
And I'll beach half these ships here at anchor,
    And these forests by me will be thinned!
I ride like a goblin and sunder
    The small lonely homes on the fell;
I will fill all your eyes with such wonder,
    For I am from hell!

Take heed and pull back from me ever
    When winter haunts seaside and shore,
For your lives I will joy then to sever
    On hillside and valley and moor.
My eyes they glow red as the embers
    In forges that fire the stars,
So redly they glow come Decembers,
    As red as red Mars.

I torment all lovers while wooing
    The kraken that sleeps in the sea.
I'll wake her with storms that I'm brewing
    Until she will love only me!
Leviathan will quarrel and fight me
    Until he is cowed by my strength;
Bleeding he'll leave but to spite me,
    Then lie at full length.

I'll trick all the lovers I find here,
    Cause dissention, pain, and discord;
I'll see that I leave them all blind here,
    Leave them frantic, venting and bored!

I'll entangle the wisdom of ages,
    I'll build each new fool his redoubt,
And smile as each pedant he rages,
    Until they pass out!

In wild storms as they pester and pillage
    I glide on the grimmest black cloud;
As these winds destroy farmland and village,
    I hover there like a dark shroud,
And glide past the oaks and the river,
    Hammer hard on the old inn's weak door,
As its dwellers gasp and they shiver,
    I move on the moor.

Moon Prayer

This moon will glow,
Its light will slant,
Such silver throw,
So elegant!
Then down dim vales
Where adders go,
On nymph-trod trails
The ghost winds blow.

Up from the scree
The gray cliffs rise
Out of the sea
Into these skies.

The night's grown cold;
I try to find
That cache of gold,
Yet I am blind.

Oh, come, my love,
And grieve me not;
My love I'll prove,
Upon this spot.
I'll kiss thee fast,
Then kiss thee slow,
To ever last,
I pray, don't go!

The Wind

I shook the walls with vigor to the end
And split the castle's ramparts into scree.
Its basalt towers toppled to the lea;
The nearby oaks and elms I break or bend.
The drawbridge, broken chains and all, descend
Into its moat now most reluctantly.
The splintered wood will wash out to the sea,
As with these manmade things I now contend.

And in my aftermath there is a hush
That haunts these shattered timbers and this stone;
Receding waters vanish in a rush.
This ruined castle's left despoiled, alone,

And I return once more from whence I came,
This all-destroying wind without a name.

Zahlore

On eves when the witches go soaring,
    And the breeze is as sharp as a blade,
As through canyons it's rushing and roaring,
    I'll stay through this night unafraid.
In those days she would visit me often,
    And oh, how I envy those years!
Her kisses my hard heart would soften,
    Now there are but tears.

Zahlore, how I've missed you and fretted,
    And sought for bought love on these coasts.
Such things I have rued and regretted,
    While I'm haunted by dull-eyed wan ghosts.
I miss both your charm and your graces,
    For you were my perfect redoubt;
I see your sweet face in all faces
    When now I go out.

I miss you so dearly and vastly,
    I will love you forever, I know;
I love you both firstly and lastly,
    Here alone in my wretched château.
I call you at high tide in winter,
    When starlight's grown weak in these skies,

As one moonbeam comes down in a splinter
    To my teary eyes.

Sweet Zahlore, so ashen and limber,
    The voice of an angel and more:
I'd grown weak with its trilling, its timbre,
    My heart like some eagle would soar!
Oh, come out of the night and the stillness,
    In a silk gown that's embroidered with red,
End all my weeping, this chillness—
    Come back from the dead!

A heretic now this remarking,
    Yet in truth I know it's absurd;
Ah, soon into death I'm embarking,
    To then fly away like some bird!
For my life now, Zahlore, it is awful,
    And with each new torture I vie,
And yet while I know it's unlawful,
    I wish to die!

On eves when the witches go soaring,
    And the breeze is as sharp as a blade,
As through canyons it's rushing and roaring,
    I'll stay through this night unafraid.
In those days she would visit me often,
    And oh, how I envy those years!
Her kisses my hard heart would soften,
    Now there are but tears.

Ingénue

She pours the jar of rare aloes about her shoulders bare,
And with a vial of galbanum she then anoints her hair,
Those rare and spicy, cool aloes bead up like crystal gems,
While on her black and fragrant hair all shine like diadems.

Now with a cotton towel she soaks those spices with a sigh,
Then up and down her legs and back until her body's dry;
She wraps her hair in turban style, the towel tucked in a fold,
Then round her waist a slender chain of thinly hammered gold.

Her eyes allure like some coiled snake that sits upon a throne,
About her gorgeous throat she hangs three torques of polished bone;
Then heavy silver in a spool she winds about each calf,
And peers into the looking-glass and lets escape a laugh.

So tall and lovely, statuesque like some pale goddess formed,
Like some rare Siren citadel by no man ever stormed,
With silken slippers now she pads adown the granite stair—
An ingénue so powerful, completely unaware.

She pours the jar of rare aloes about her shoulders bare,
And with a vial of galbanum she then anoints her hair,
Those rare and spicy, cool aloes bead up like crystal gems,
While on her black and fragrant hair all shine like diadems.

The Muse

Far from environs of our boiling sun,
She fled from me to realms ineffable,
To silken seas whose restless tides foretell
The waking of some new Leviathan.
Where lurching mountains, mauve and cinnamon,
Throw shadows on the moorland and the fell,
Where grows the amaranth and asphodel,
It's here she leaves me to oblivion.

And yet within my deepest black despair,
When all is lost and I am faced with doom,
I know her scent, thick in the midnight air,
Her rare and most enchanting strong perfume.
Then I grow giddy and all my head's aswirl—
She has come back, my Muse, my fickle girl!

The Upper Air

Starkly, coolly,
Meanly, cruelly,
Is this woman made.
Love her duly,
Kindly, smoothly,
Still I am afraid.
She will scold thee,
Bend and fold thee,

In the midnight shade.
Break thee, rake thee,
Drain and take thee,
Wanton, not a maid.
Holding, clinging,
Sorrow bringing,
Darkness in her eyes,
She will play thee,
Sway and slay thee,
Till the red dawn rise.
Slowly, wholly,
Dark, unholy,
She will lay thee there.
Redly, deadly,
She'll not wed thee
In the upper air.

The Inconstant Lover

Beyond this moor and haunted fell,
I seek mine ancient pain to quell,
Then to the dark I softly tell:
Come out, Michelle, come out, Michelle!

And by this ancient witch-cursed fen
I move, the loneliest of men,
I whisper once and then again:
Sweet Madeleine, sweet Madeleine!

Beyond this mist I hear the sea,
Its tides drone on eternally,
There echoes seem to shout to me:
Lost Stephanie, lost Stephanie!

My heart now rising to a roar,
Above me birds of omen soar,
And then that voice that I adore,
My sweet Zahlore, my sweet Zahlore!

The Sorcerer Fashions a Lover for Himself

On these moons of red Mars that go swirling,
    It orbits elliptic and bold,
I watch as these comets go hurling
    With detritus, ice and with gold.
And they fly past so quickly while screaming,
    Like the ring of a sad silent bell,
While I'm busy both working and scheming
    And casting a spell.

I fashion a woman of pleasure,
    A girl of a magic device,
And I make her for love without measure,
    With a heart that is hard as is ice.
For she's meant for me and me only,
    As I fashion her here on this shore:
She's my drug for all that is lonely,
    My paramour!

She is tall and aloof and most charming,
    And her love is meant only for me;
Her beauty is stunning, disarming,
    Like some goddess emerged from the sea.
Her eyes are huge pools of lost magic,
    Her smooth flesh is as pale as a pearl;
Her smile is most sensual, tragic,
    A godlike young girl.

Her legs are as long as the winter
    In the climes that are noted for cold;
Her beauty could shatter and splinter
    Great kingdoms by armies patrolled.
Her hair is a sea like red oceans,
    Her curves most alluring and sly;
She is laved in sweet spices and lotions,
    No strain on the eye!

She's a marvel and challenging lover,
    A girl who is learnéd in love;
She will love me alone, like no other,
    My pampered most magical dove!
She will love with the strength of a lion,
    Her kiss like a soft summer's breeze;
I will ride with her then to Orion,
    On its methane seas.

She stands here a thing most resplendent,
    A girl who might rule or command;
Her beauty angelic, transcendent,
    All made by my sorcerer's hand!

She waits till my words I have spoken,
    And obeys me as fast as she might;
No command has she ever now broken,
    This goddess of night!

Cassandra I named her at dawning,
    When Mars was in zenith and then,
There in that sky's starry awning,
    She became the seducer of men!
Yet this was much more than I wanted,
    Ah, but her beauty would shine!
So now on occasion I'm haunted,
    Although she is mine!

She'll not age nor any blade scar her,
    She's immortal as might be some god;
No physical thing may now mar her
    Or her lovely and gorgeous façade!
Yet now on occasion she's sneering,
    Or so I think I have seen;
And lately I find myself fearing—
    What might this mean?

Could my lover turn hateful and savage?
    Could she harm her strong lover and king?
No! For she's special, not average,
    I refuse to accept such a thing!
Cassandra's turned pouty and troubled,
    And her pretty head she will hang low,
And her obstinacy somehow has doubled!
    A most fatal blow.

I decided to kill her one twilight,
    Right here in this dark shadowed hall,
Where two moons cast a subtle strong highlight
    There on my high granite wall.
She laughed till I thought she was crying,
    And called me a jaded old fool;
With spells most outré sent me dying
    With my blood in a pool!

I bled till my soul fled my castle:
    Cassandra was joyous and laughed!
"I am shed of that wretched old vassal!"
    She sang as some fine wine she quaffed.
She brought in a stable of lovers,
    And my wines she abundantly poured.
All her loves were short-lived, as all others. . . .
    I silently roared!

My Cassandra's turned brutish, still pretty,
    And as crude as a sailor and more;
Her speech has turned savage, not witty,
    Yet she still has that magic allure!
The years they drift by, yet she's ageless,
    And her lovers are numbered like grass;
Yet the book of her true love is pageless,
    Unhappy young lass.

The Offering

Few loves like this love in my heart is,
That fills both this headland and lea,
For my love a most guileless art is
As vast as this chill constant sea.
And my heart is a grail and a token
That I hold and I offer to thee—
A love most secure and unbroken
As sure as this cold savage sea.

My castles for thee I've anointed,
Their walls made of granite and steel,
With seneschals duly appointed
To obey thee with ardor and zeal.
My galleys all anchored now leeward,
Where these loons at noontime will flee;
At your word my ships move out seaward,
To take you across this chill sea.

And in ports where my cities await thee,
They have gathered mulled wine for the cold,
Rare wines to amuse or sedate thee,
In goblets of silver or gold.
My slave girls I've tasked with a duty,
To attend to and comfort but thee;
They are young and renowned for their beauty,
To lavish thee here by this sea!

In palaces raised for thy pleasure
Whose walls are all builded of gneiss,
I will love thee here without measure
And treasure your tiniest kiss!
My chests are all opened, each offers
Jewels from far over this sea.
They are yours! Yes, all of these coffers,
As well as all else just for thee!

The Pretty Jinn

On some lost ramp
Deep down the dell
I found a lamp,
And sensed a spell—
A spell that could
Drive storms across
The moor and wood,
Or conjure loss.

I from black sands
Wiped it across,
And with my hands
Removed the moss.
Then she rose up,
A lovely thing;
From that brass cup
She'd speak and sing.

Gold at her throat,
Neat as a pin,
And there she'd float
This pretty jinn.
More golden bands,
As I would stare,
Above her hands,
Her flesh most bare.

One pretty ear
From night-black hair
Caused love and fear
In that night air.
We sat and spoke,
For some long while;
Her hair I'd stroke,
Her heart pure guile.

Now rotted bone
Of little worth,
Lies there alone
Within the that earth,
I'm here to tell
Stay far away
Else that jinn's spell
Might thee, too, slay.

An Encounter at Dusk

I saw her in the dusk one eve,
    She filled me with such awe.
A beast of myth that few believe—
    Outside the natural law.

She was part mare, and stripèd, sleek,
    Long hair of scented black;
She held a curving bow of teak,
    Her hair fell down her back.

Her eyes were otherworldly, dark,
    Her torso tinged with peach;
Her gaze held some fantastic spark,
    Such magics she might teach!

She was a deadly archer there,
    And pranced like one assured.
Strong perfumes then would scent that air—
    I'm sure she was adored.

So beautiful, yet deadly, sweet,
    Her fetlocks muscled, long;
She had four hooves instead off feet—
    Her smile might summon dawn.

Her eyes were fay, no human eyes
    Had ever shone this bright;
Then on rear legs I saw her rise
    And flee into the night.

Three Kisses

This star's coruscations, its glow and its eye
     Here cast silver light on the fell.
This October is cold and these grasslands all dry,
As a pretty pale ghost sighs out her sweet sigh,
     Her beauty the dead might impel.

She moves like one living, a nubile young teen,
     Her hair is part red and part gold;
A willowy thing most exceedingly lean,
She shouts to me boldly that her name is Jean,
     By swarms of odd mist she's patrolled.

Her eyes are quite large and as gray as the seas
     That haunt all this bay and the reef;
Her hair is most lovely and sways in the breeze,
She seems one with the stars, the moon and these trees,
     Yet she holds some lost secret grief.

Her white skirt is too short and her legs are too long,
     Her movements enchantment itself!
She speaks to me slyly, her words like some song,
She offers to stay with me here till the dawn,
     This curious sweet little elf!

I'm polite but demure, and I say I must go,
     That my family waits near yonder hill.
She smiles and three kisses to me she'll bestow,
To my eyes and my lips, one, two, three in a row—
     She's lovely yet terribly chill!

She says she's sweet Jean, and she knows she's a ghost,
    She comes up when Orion is nigh;
She laughs and she whispers she loves me the most!
I smile and I tell her go back to the coast;
    She is sad, but her smile is most sly!

This star's coruscations, its glow and its eye
    Here cast silver light on the fell.
This October is cold and these grasslands all dry,
As a pretty pale ghost sighs out her sweet sigh,
    Her beauty the dead might impel.

Sarah Jane

This night once more has called you forth
    To walk this lane
Of brothels stretching South to North,
    Sweet Sarah Jane.

Tall and winsome, most robust,
    Both lovely, vain;
You walk to quench unsated lust,
    Proud Sarah Jane.

Too many times you've led me there,
    Yes, just we twain.
I've gloried in your luscious hair,
    Sly Sarah Jane.

And yet my heart you've caught, and hold,
    Though I'm not fain
To let you know. I'm not so bold,
    No, Sarah Jane.

This night I watch you once again,
    And I feel pain
That you now know so many men,
    Dark Sarah Jane.

Perhaps if I . . . but I'm no fool,
    That ball and chain
You nightly don has made you cruel,
    My Sarah Jane.

And so I smile and offer cash;
    You don't complain,
But smile at me, blue eyes you flash,
    Bright Sarah Jane.

You walk with me like some old friend;
    In your domain
You're always kind, my words attend,
    Sweet Sarah Jane.

We speak of things we've done before,
    And they contain
The germ of love, which you ignore,
    Smart Sarah Jane!

And then one night you did not come.
    They would explain:

You left with him. I was struck dumb
> By Sarah Jane.

I was not bold, nor was I brave,
> But soft, mundane.

I'll curse myself until the grave
> For Sarah Jane.

Above the Fallen Gate

Undesecrate my love retains
Its strength across the old estate
Where weeds grow tall upon these lanes,
> Undesecrate.

The château's walls are now prostrate;
Our chambers subject to the rains,
Long gone our gold and silverplate.

My pale ghost nightly yet maintains
Its watch above the fallen gate.
You see, my love, it still remains
> Undesecrate!

Where Shadows Weave

Where shadows weave against the sill
On moonless nights below the eave,
I hear the mournful whippoorwill
> Where shadows weave.

It's on such nights I sigh and grieve,
As winds stir up a sudden chill;
Her ghost sometimes I then perceive.

These cloistered stars may then distill
The magic of her rustled sleeve,
The softest sound as all lies still,
    Where shadows weave.

The Ghost of Guinevere

To lay a ghost I called a seer
So long regarded as the most
Renowned of mages far or near,
    To lay a ghost.

He came to man that spirit's post
Within my castle dim and drear;
He waxed loquacious, full of boast.

Then she came forth, her wan left ear
Pierced with brown topaz from the coast.
We failed with lovely Guinevere
    To lay a ghost.

Cold Love

When love grows cold there will arise
Fell shadows hulking, so I'm told,

To blot out sun and stars and skies
    When love grows cold.

And though I've carefully patrolled
My love, that is my fondest prize,
I've lost her who is more than gold.

Why is it that lost love and lies
Are as thrown dice by dead hands rolled?
These tears run hot from my sad eyes
    When love grows cold.

Haunted Château

Through some soft subtle magic strangely willed,
I watched the pale pellucid pied ghosts race
To chambers lapped in long and lovely lace;
Upon some crimson-crafted carpet spilled
Odd onyx orbs, and ashy opals filled
The fluted floors with finery and grace.
The purple pall of twilight purged the place,
A wild white wine of witchery distilled.

I watched a cold cabal of ghosts confer,
Though soaked in sorcery and spells. "Beware!"
I cried to chimeras that came to stir
That mantic moiling moonlight on the stair.
Swift sable secret spells were shattered there,
To veer and vanish in that vaunted air.

To Wake the Dead

Down halls with copper railings
    Where few men ever tread,
The dusk brings banshee wailings,
    Enough to wake the dead.
The candles' dripping tallow
    Drips on this dusty floor;
They cast light poor and sallow,
    As creaks the brass-hinged door.

Wan ghosts now flit so quickly
    Through window slit and hall;
With smoke the air's grown thickly,
    As savage shadows sprawl.
So powerful and starkly,
    A girl appears before,
As night has fallen darkly
    There by the brass-hinged door.

Now hoofs sound in the stable,
    Yet there no horses are.
The dark has grown twice sable,
    Lit by an evil star;
With sanguine spirits hiding,
    This girl spreads out her arms—
Male spirits swooning, gliding,
    Allured by her vast charms.

She's pale and lean and straining

    To rule this hall again;
Presiding, entertaining,
    She owns the hearts of men.
Her gown is overflowing,
    Her silks trail in the dust,
Her tempting eyes now glowing,
    Her heart all burning lust.

Down halls with copper railings
    Where few men ever tread,
The dusk brings banshee wailings,
    Enough to wake the dead.
The candles' dripping tallow
    Drips on this dusty floor;
They cast light poor and sallow,
    As creaks the brass-hinged door.

Raquel

These whispered words have called you forth:
    Each is a spell
Of magic from the icy North,
    My pale Raquel.

In valleys where the glaciers roll,
    No abbey bell
Could stanch the words that made you whole,
    My tall Raquel.

Some ancient wizard bored with life
    Could not foretell
That you were no mere conjure wife—
    Not you, Raquel!

You slew him when the full moon's phase
    Began to swell:
That tale you've twisted in these days.
    A lie, Raquel!

You took his castle, roof to pave,
    And there you dwell;
Your heart is hollow as the grave,
    My dark Raquel.

And when the snows these valleys fill,
    Your love you sell
To hapless men you woo and kill,
    My proud Raquel.

Yet I have lived to tell the tale,
    For I rebel
Against your beauty filled with bale,
    My wan Raquel.

We danced within your winter hall:
    How you excel
When darkness comes and shadows fall
    On you, Raquel.

You slipped your noose and made it fast;
    I'm now a shell.
Yet I escaped there at the last
    From you, Raquel.

But every night my dreams are torn,
    For you compel
That I forever be forlorn,
    Oh, dark Raquel!

Ah, now this pistol is my friend,
    I bid farewell;
My miseries are at an end,
    Adieu, Raquel.

Moon Love

I sought the skull-like, wan, occludent moon,
Yet wandering clouds hung heavy in that sky.
Here spirits shook the cane stalks and the rye;
Their icy whispers echoed, each a rune,
To charm the sun from out the sky at noon,
Or conjure Sirens with a single sigh;
Yet still I sought the night's huge opal eye
And prayed that I would see it shining soon.

Then pretty ghosts came up out of the ground:
Each wore a lovely, slinky, silver dress!
They lolled and knelt and gathered all around;

One tried to soothe me with her cold caress.
I paid no heed, yet stared and stared above:
I seek the moon, she is my only love.

The Ghost Train

I dreamed that out across the plains
    I heard the whistle scream;
I knew full well there were no trains,
    That this was just a dream.

The night was cold, the moon hung low,
    It snowed in sand-like grain;
But here I watched the blizzard blow,
    Quite safe within the train.

I sat within an antique car
    From eighteen ninety-two;
I blew my fists, the cold to bar,
    My cowboy hat askew.

For I was marshal of a town
    Whose name is lost to men;
I was a man of great renown
    Who rides this train again.

And like a ghost across the plain,
    Once more the blizzard howled;
I sat my bench aboard the train,
    Looked at the scene and scowled.

And then it was the train it slowed,
    Stopped in this stormy strife,
But still it snowed and snowed and snowed;
    The engine roared to life.

Again it was we rode the rails,
    But then a man appeared:
He, stern and lean and tough as nails;
    He wore no hat or beard.

An Indian, out of the blue,
    Came out that icy air;
There was no doubt he was a Sioux,
    One feather in his hair.

He looked at me with eyes of pain,
    And hatred in his gaze;
He sat him down there on that train,
    A ghost, a smoky haze.

He spoke in words like thunder's call,
    And cursed me with disdain.
He'd come back down death's long dark hall
    To ride aboard this train.

He told me things I'd heard before;
    I listened to him drone.
He was quite easy to ignore
    In muffled monotone.

He stopped, rolled up his eyes, and sighed,
    And I could see his pain.
I told him that I thought he'd lied,
    And please get off the train.

Again he rolled his eyes and sighed,
    And smiled like he was Cain.
"It is tonight that you have died:
    That's why you ride this train!"

The blizzard howled like roaring hell,
    While I could not refrain
From cursing whistle and the bell,
    Aboard the blizzard train.

Aphasia

These stars have marked me as their own to burn away to ash.
My elfin love, her heart was stone: to love her was most rash.
She came from headlands long unknown; she came to lure me in.
Her love's a blade that she can hone: we grappled there in sin.

My sweet Aphasia, aptly named, you poisoned love's sharp dart.
I stand now naked, ill, ashamed: thou fiend, you've pierced my heart!
Oh, savage girl, my love you claimed, there on that fateful day.
Aphasia, I've been wrongly blamed, and been sent far away.

Aphasia, thou art deeply tanned, so smooth is thy flesh.
You leave me broken and unmanned! My heart and soul enmesh!
Thy dagger's thrust, right from the start, was harsh as harsh can be:
You pierced with steel my pulsing heart and took the life from me.

My lovely pixie, slyly styled, with wings of gossamer:
I am ashamed, and spent, defiled—it's all because of her!
Aphasia, how your love beguiled, called stars from out the sky!
My cairn stones now so crudely piled, for here it is I'll die.

The Fire Fairy

If dreams might grow much darker,
I'd care not to see more,
For while she is quite charming,
There something most disarming:
The fire fairy's darker
Than all who went before.
If dreams might grow much darker,
I'd care not to see more.

A gown of golden leather,
Her hands of magma made,
Her gray eyes most disturbing,
Her beauty strange, perturbing,
And in her hair a feather,
Tied to a flaxen braid:
A gown of golden leather
Her hands of magma made.

Her lips spoke of desire,
Her pretty nails pale jade.
No girl was so precocious,
Pretty or ferocious,

She plays with conjured fire.
Her lust none can evade,
Her lips spoke of desire,
Her pretty nails pale jade.

Her ears so long and pointed,
She took me in her arms;
The laws of dream defying,
I shouted, crying, dying.
Her kiss my face anointed,
And quelled each man's alarms;
Her ears so long and pointed,
She took me in her arms.

If dreams might grow much darker,
I'd care not to see more,
For while she is quite charming,
There something most disarming
The fire fairy's darker,
Than all who went before.
If dreams might grow much darker,
I'd care not to see more.

All Hallows Eve

On nights when the ghouls are out culling
    This march by the haunted château,
As the witches there, sullenly sculling,
    Embark with their black spells in tow,

I've come out of my cave in the mountains
    Through valleys now swollen with rain,
Till the roads look like meres or strange fountains,
    And yet I am fain.

I move with the wind as it whispers,
    Or I'll slink with the shadows that fall
So hard by the abbey at vespers,
    Or I'll vault some old castle's high wall,
Or I'll float with those vapors now spewing
    From lawns near the farms by the moor,
A place that all men are eschewing
    That I yet adore!

I tap at dark windows. A sleeper
    Now may hear my low voice in the night,
And if she's a girl I will seek her
    In dreams fraught with terror and fright.
I may spool to the highest church steeple
    That is covered with thick rust and moss:
Though I'm unafraid of all people,
    I do fear the Cross!

It's back to the brambles and thistles,
    Near the hedge row that twists round the lane;
I can hear the dead reeds as each whistles
    In this lea that spreads out toward the plain.
Now ennui has assaulted my senses,
    As I turn for my far distant tor,

And I fly over courtyards and fences:
  This world's such a bore!

On nights when the ghouls are out culling
  This march by the haunted château,
As the witches there, sullenly sculling,
  Embark with their black spells in tow,
I've come out of my cave in the mountains,
  Through valleys now swollen with rain,
Till the roads look like meres or strange fountains,
  And yet I am fain.

Phantom Wife

Thou art slender,
  And you can
True love render
  For this man.
Seeming fragile,
  Small and spare;
Strong and agile
  Like a bear!

Girl of bold dreams,
  Young and sweet;
Over cold streams
  Swift and fleet.
Woo me under
  These dark stars:

Full of wonder,
 Love is ours!

Gently breathing
 Your sweet breath,
My soul seething,
 Unto death!
You have honed me
 Like a knife,
Loved and own me,
 Phantom wife.

Through the brushes,
 Through the ferns,
Your love hushes,
 My love burns!
Hold me tighter:
 I may swoon,
Thou art brighter
 Than this moon!

Gift of kisses
 For thy brow,
Know what bliss is,
 Know it now!
Love combining
 With a kiss,
Cling, entwining,
 Just like this!

Bewitched and Beguiled

The spell of her kisses, her breathtaking sighs,
    They fill her with grace and allure.
And I'm pierced by the ravenous look in her eyes;
She's an angel of Love, who now guards paradise.
    She's a girl that all men adore.

Her hair is an ocean as red as red Mars,
    As it moves in its orbit quite cold;
She's pursued constantly by male avatars,
A daughter to kings and a sister to stars
    That flame with the brightest bright gold!

She walks like the alders that sway in the breeze,
    And her movements all perfectly mesh;
I'm drunk with her scent as it floats on the breeze,
My pale anxious lover who rules all the seas—
    And like down is her creamy white flesh.

On worlds that revolve around moons and a sun,
    She is princess of all she can see.
Into her arms like some madman I run;
I am crushed by her beauty, completely undone,
    That she finds but one moment for me!

A goddess perhaps from the outlands of old,
    That no man may recall in this year?
Our hearts and emotions she's always controlled;
About her are spirits that long have patrolled,
    So she walks now abroad without fear.

A princess of pearls and of lavender spells,
    This witch girl she chants a soft rune.
Her magic informs and bewitches, compels,
As her beauty enchants, entices, impels,
    Below this romantical moon.

Her crown is a crown of smelted pure gold
    From richest and rarest of ores.
There's no luxury that her lovers withhold—
We woo her with ardor, incredibly bold,
    Here on these wan moonlit shores.

A Siren, perhaps, from the cold briny deep
    Who enchants us with spells most outré?
I vision a castle where high in its keep,
Where she lies all alone in a deep dreamless sleep,
    Above some fantastic lost bay.

She's queen of these were-beasts that wander the moor
    When the moon is a wan risen jewel;
They cower before her, and yet they adore
This girl they beseech and respect and implore;
    And yet she's tyrannically cruel.

The harpies above her, they scream out their fear,
    As the avatars kneel at her side.
The moon's now occluded, the night has grown drear,
And now a bold vampire approaches quite near
    And begs her to be his own bride!

A daughter to lions, the witch of the world,
    A girl who is human and more!
I grow weak as each tress is now curled and uncurled,
And faint at her hair, a red banner unfurled,
    And I love her as never before!

A sorceress sure with impeccable nails
    Painted red like the daggers of doom;
Her love is a weapon that always prevails,
A vessel of beauty, the grail of all grails,
    While her kisses, they banish all gloom.

A Siren, like Circe, she charms every man;
    Like Ulysses they're cowed by her love.
It seems she was born when this old world began—
She was borne by her slaves on a bone-white divan,
    While of magics she knows all thereof.

Her suitors, all maddened, can do little more
    But to rave like one who's gone wild;
They sigh and they groan and they'll sprawl on the floor
And plead for the love of this fay paramour,
    Who seems but a bold willful child!

They prostrate themselves, of their love will they sing,
    And she'll step on a wretched man's neck!
She's as bold as pure brass, with the strength of a king,
As we suitors, like fools, to her gown hems all cling,
    And each one of us now is a wreck.

At the nod of her head her suitors will tense
    And try then to guess her least whim;
She's hypnotized all and she's banished good sense,
For this her sad suitors will pay recompense—
    The outlook for them is most grim.

Yet she coddles me like the fool that I am,
    And she smiles at my heavy sad sigh.
Though I've slain fifty brigands, I'm merely a lamb:
My importance to her is also a sham,
    And someday she will leave me to die!

The spell of her kisses her breathtaking sighs,
    They fill her with grace and allure.
And I'm pierced by the ravenous look in her eyes;
She's an angel of Love who now guards paradise.
    She's a girl that all men adore.

Gray Eyes

The weary loons on sea walls sleep this eve,
Near shadows that these headlands cast.
And from the sand an ancient rotted mast
Points starward as the ebbing tides now leave.
It's here the sea its ancient magics weave
Where ghost ships ply from out the distant Past,
While buoy bells ring across the icy vast
Where sea and stars and land all interweave.

It's here, at dusk, I think of my Marie,
Her strange gray eyes, the magic scent of myrrh
Mixed with the briny cogent restless sea—
All these that made me fall a slave to her;
Yet that was long ago, and she's now gone.
I wait, alone, for nothing but the dawn.

Street Walker

Her beauty makes all suitors gawk and stammer,
    All eyes grow wide to stare;
When she walks on the street there is a clamor,
    A goddess with red hair.

Her kiss so lethal will enthrall, enamor,
    For she is passing fair;
Now each man's heart will pound like some steel hammer
    For one so debonair.

Her beauty from some dark magician's grammar,
    Deep in his hidden lair;
He conjured her with some amazing glamour
    From water and the air.

All love her from the first time that they scan her,
    As lovely as a prayer;
Yet though her love is bought I do not damn her,
    Cold harlot of despair.

The Silver Pin

My little lover is the twin
Of angels soaring in the skies,
And in her huge and steel-gray eyes
Brims all the love of Lillian.

I watch her barefoot in the halls
Twirl thin fingers in the air,
Brush back her long and yellow hair
Till like a cloak of gold it falls.

She wears two rings of polished tin;
Her nut-brown throat, by sunlight kissed,
Sports three thin torques of amethyst.
This pleases my fay Lillian.

And through her soft silk slits her thighs
Peek out when gentle breezes swirl:
A Siren is my laughing girl,
Though sometimes she is full of sighs.

Her voice is like some violin,
Made from a wood not of this Earth;
Her smile is full of guileless mirth—
This is my lovely Lillian.

On her bare hips a golden chain
Was by a master goldsmith knit:
Like gossamer so delicate,
She wears her pretty chatelaine.

And now with one long silver pin
She gently sweeps up all her hair,
And with that pin she holds it there,
Then goes to sleep, my Lillian.

The Wicked Girl

This wicked girl led me astray:
    She'd fallen far from grace.
She favored night, she said, not day;
    Her top was tatted lace.
While something in her scent, her sway,
    And in her angel's face
Most eagerly would let me pay
    One night in her embrace.

She was petite and pretty, spare;
    Said, "I'm your paramour!"
Then took my hand and up the stair
    She led me to her door;
And giddy from her scented hair
    My heart would pulse and roar,
And in a trice we then were there
    And crossed her hardwood floor.

Such sin I know is vile and base,
    And vague my memory,
And yet within that perfumed place
    I drowned as in a sea.

She was an unrelenting tide
    That thrashed me loud and long;
She was that eve my warm faux bride
    Who stayed with me till dawn.

Then I returned within the week,
    And yet there was no trace;
No matter how I'd try or seek,
    Or dreamed of her white lace.
Yet all was gone, save her mystique,
    With just my own disgrace;
She somehow seemed now most antique,
    A girl long out of place.

The years have gathered into piles,
    My hair is like to snow;
And so well I recall her wiles,
    The magic they'd bestow.
I dream of her upon her stairs,
    As lovely as a doe,
And all my dreams are full of prayers,
    And pray that she will know.

The Ghost Bell

I heard the ghost bell sound one eve
At low tide from the ruined kirk
Where no bell was, so by your leave
I climbed atop the steep-walled cirque.

Myself I pulled hand over hand;
The winds whipped, oh, so mightily,
But ghostly eyes soon saw me stand
Before that kirk ringed by the sea.

Once more I heard that ghostly chime,
Its iron echoes deftly flung:
Seemed like some challenge given Time,
To peal out anger when it rung.

Its dark tones stiff and cutting, harsh,
My very blood would cloy and freeze!
It echoed there down to the marsh,
An iron curse upon the breeze.

I looked to find that great bronze tongue:
No bell I found, where it should be,
But only niches where it hung
Here, long ago, above the sea.

I heard the ghost bell sound one eve
At low tide from the ruined kirk
Where no bell was, so by your leave
I climbed atop the steep-walled cirque.

An Iron Gong

Down winding alleys in this ancient port
I've traveled in a drugged and deathlike sleep.
The moon hangs low above a weathered keep
Where waiting is my amorous consort.

Its wooden door cannot my passions thwart—
I smash this door and up those stairs I sweep
To find my love and untold pleasures reap,
And through the night the two of us cavort.

An iron gong sounds from a minaret.
My lover shifts her shape and is no more
An eager young and nubile pale brunette.
She's now become a thing to shun, abhor,
As through the windows bitter breezes blow,
She spreads bat wings and flies, with me in tow!

Dark Paramour

Here under tall oaks in her garden
    Where so long she has lured only fools,
Her resolve she enflames and will harden,
    Like hot magma as it slowly cools.
Now over the storm-haunted headland,
    Far under the tusk of the moon,
I yet wander so lost in this dead land,
    Both night and at noon.

Dead specters are endlessly roaming
    On the eves that mark their demise;
They are seen on her shores in the gloaming
    As they stare with their pale opaque eyes.
She casts her strong spells on the mountains,
    Far down the glades through the leas;

Stone seneschals stand by her fountains
    To stare at the seas.

Like a tall young reed, supple, slender,
    Or like aspens that sway in the breeze,
Her beauty can lull and can render
    You unconscious, your very soul freeze.
She's nubile and facile, most cunning,
    With potions and aloes she's laved;
Her beauty's intense and twice stunning,
    All lovers are scathed.

Her gold citadels shine in the thunder
    During storms that blow in from the West;
Here she's scheming new ways she can sunder
    This poor heart that still beats in my breast.
Try as I might I will stumble,
    For she breathes in the rarest of air;
Before her are all men made humble,
    From here to Altair.

In strange fanes in her cities I've wandered,
    On dark nights when I've drunk to the gods;
Such hours with her have I squandered
    And survived against all of the odds.
Her talismans, spells unbecoming—
    She's more lovely than Venus of old—
We're all helpless as each one's succumbing
    To kisses like gold.

Like the Sirens who lured with their kisses
    On the seas where the Greeks sailed and roamed,
I feel like some latter Ulysses
    On these shores where the breakers long foamed.
Over and under the ages
    I am pulled and I'm turned as I go;
My lover's a cruel witch who rages,
    With me now in tow.

Her love and her ardor so taxes
    My poor heart as I hide in the shade,
I am like an oak felled with axes—
    For my dalliance well have I paid!
Her magics beyond all sane measure,
    There's such guile in her tiniest curl,
This princess of pain and of pleasure,
    This magical girl.

Now span on great span of the star-streams
    Has covered me like a dark tomb;
For she is the one who can bar dreams
    Or enchant you with sighs and perfume.
She's broken the spell of the wizards
    With strange ores she has plucked from the sun,
And stanched all her foes with harsh blizzards
    To oblivion!

Her towers are thick-walled and olden,
    Raised up by dead kings of the past;

Her turrets all silver and golden,
    Her courtyards all granite and vast.
Her windows all opal and garnet,
    And she sighs at the beauty she's known,
This Jezebel lovely, incarnate,
    Whose heart is as stone.

On fields where her worst foes all die on,
    In great battles that raged until dawn,
Now ghost armies from Edo to Sion
    March nightly till morn when they're gone.
Their bones bleach hard by these beaches,
    Where their ships were all snagged on the reef;
Now their spirits wail here to the reaches,
    All, all unto grief.

In towers all builded of sorrow,
    She will call up a prince or a swain;
These sad fools they will die on the marrow,
    By her manicured hand are they slain.
Each night there is plenteous laughter,
    And her songs, which sound like some rune,
Will echo from donjon to rafter
    Far under the moon.

The horizon is thick with her galleys,
    Her tall quinqueremes carry such gain;
From her tower she lazily tallies
    Gold brought in from the lost mines of Spain.

Triremes with their long oars are rowing,
    Their great holds bearing spices and myrrh,
As fair winds in their sails are now blowing
    These ships unto her.

On eves when the moon seems a beacon
    Under star-streams of purple and red,
Her smile so allures and can weaken
    And seemingly call up the dead.
Hold back your charms, my sweet spellcaster,
    Let storm clouds here block out the moon;
One kiss from your lips is disaster—
    I fall in a swoon.

Her fleets come in Junes and Septembers,
    When the moon is a blade in the night,
And she broods and she smiles and remembers
    Her power and wealth with delight.
On rivers like Ob and the Yangtze,
    Her long barges ply out from the East;
On Nile and Euphrates, Zambezi,
    Bring foods for a feast.

Her lovers like cattle she's herded
    Into pens, this maleficent daughter;
With sweet songs so cunningly worded,
    She's led them like lambs to the slaughter.
Though breezy and lovely and scented
    With rare myrrh and the finest aloes,

She is cold, and so harsh, unrepented,
    A most lethal rose!

So long have I searched and I've striven,
    Seeking solace while catching my breath,
While all my vain efforts you've riven,
    And forcing me closer to death.
Your love is like a sweet gallows
    That towers above me and then;
Your kisses are stale, each unhallows
    The lives of all men.

I will fast and pray in her garden,
    And seek God's forgiveness once more,
And pray that her heart will unharden,
    My most sensuous dark paramour.
So under these oaks I am trying
    All her sins and mine to amend;
I'm through with deception and lying,
    And know it must end.

Her eyes in the dusk so like embers,
    As she waits by the fruit bearing lime,
She is dreaming and always remembers
    The lovers she pulled out of Time.
Her frown like a riptide will sunder
    Your life and your soul from the start;
Her anger like Zeus-driven thunder
    That will break your heart.

Now I try in these barren regions
    Her ramparts to breach and to storm,
But she slays my war-hardened legions
    And leads me to ultimate harm.
She is winsome and guileful and clever,
    While her love is a razor-sharp blade,
And with it she'll dice you and sever,
    Duplicitous maid!

Her evil can startle and chasten,
    Yet too late for her lovers to save
Their lives though they scramble and hasten,
    They are buried, unmarked, in a grave.
Now we've tangled and tumbled and shouted,
    From midnight to dawn upon dawn,
Yet naught is to her once she's pouted,
    Or rendered a yawn.

Una Sandoval

Aldebaran winked evilly as all
The faded stars made way for Luna's eye.
The field was filled with one lone loon's sad cry,
While there was something brooding overall.
Hard by the tomb of Una Sandoval,
A sorceress who ruled the Eastern sky,
From Baja to the slums of old Shanghai
Her spirit cast a dreary twilight pall.

* * *

Yet I recall a meadow in the spring
Where we would sit and pluck the daisies there;
Though I was poor she made me feel a king,
I'd place those daisies in her scented hair.
So when I come to visit her lone tomb,
My memories then banish all the gloom.

Frankenstein

High in my castle tower
    I took the liches there,
To build a man of power,
    If not quite debonair.
I sewed him up like leather
    And gave him one huge brain,
Then waited for the weather,
    Both lightning and rain.

I laid him on a stretcher
    I fashioned from rough pine;
With rods, a lightning catcher,
    I built by design.
His life flowed, he went twitching!
    Here rose a thing malign,
And all my plans went glitching,
    Where shambled Frankenstein!

Ghost Rider

Strange spells unaccounted;
    A wind from the fen.
A ghost steed unmounted
    By spirits of men.

This air is unsteady
    In gathering gloom;
It swirls in an eddy
    Above my stone tomb.

Down in the valley
    The grotto is still;
Here wan spirits rally
    Beside a cold rill.

I'm game for the gloaming,
    I'm swift as a doe;
For soon I'll be roaming
    Across this plateau.

My lovers uncounted,
    All grist for the mill;
That steed I've now mounted,
    We ride with a will!

Now on these swift breezes
    We garner our strength;
Our power the sea's is,
    We ride its full length.

These mermaids in wonder,
    They stare and they stare;
With steel hooves of thunder
    We trample the air!

Away into weather
    We ride all the day,
Then circle the heather,
    Then circle the bay.

Cassandra is calling—
    She's eager for me;
Her absence is galling,
    As galling can be.

Cassandra, I'm coming,
    And soon will be there;
My poor heart's loud drumming
    Now fills all the air.

Strange spells unaccounted,
    A wind from the fen,
A ghost steed unmounted
    By spirits men.

A Nightmare

    Dreams of others,
    Time-lost lovers
Rush by me like a silver stream;
    Catch me crying
    Sad and sighing,
For well I know it's but a dream.

    I yet hope in
    Love to open
Across this heather in the rain;
    It is fruitless,
    Worse than useless
To hold in fief this biting pain.

    Watch when Mars is
    Under stars is
Swift moving through Orion's Belt.
    Then she'll whisper,
    Tempting sister,
There at her shrine where long I've knelt.

    Lost dominions,
    Evil minions
Race me to my nightmare's door;
    None exempting
    Sorely tempting
Me from my sweet paramour.

Selene

Such gold and garnets grace your form,
    Both pale, pristine;
Your beauty's far beyond the norm,
    My coy Selene.

Your bracelets are of silver made,
    Fit for a queen;
So opulent are they displayed
    On you Selene.

The opals in your ears rejoice
    As you careen,
As though they hang of their own choice,
    My fay Selene.

All men grow weak and give a gasp;
    They are most keen
To hold you in a steely grasp,
    My sly Selene!

How like a goddess on the mall
    Who stands between
Both life and death. Exceptional
    Are you, Selene!

Quite pert and agile, never staid;
    No figurine
Are you, my sweet coquettish maid—
    No, not Selene!

Cool as the autumn are your eyes,
    Yet you're unclean;
You've been with many men who prize
    You so, Selene.

They pay in script or coin to learn
    What others glean:
That lovers for you ever burn,
    My dark Selene.

Your flesh most supple, soft, and pale
    As is baleen;
Thou art a most corrupted grail,
    My sweet Selene!

Oft times exotic, then jejune,
    Yes, and obscene,
Though still a goddess of the moon,
    My sad Selene.

A regal touch, beyond my ken;
    A royal mien
You have, that tempts so many men,
    Countess Selene!

You'd charm the gods of stone and brass
    Who there convene
Before their fanes upon the grass—
    Yes, you, Selene.

Just when I think your anger's spent—
    You're often mean—
You snap me like some twig you've bent,
    Oh, cruel Selene!

I'm little more than your sad toy,
    As you've foreseen,
For naught to you is man or boy,
    Twice-harsh Selene!

As ages come and ages go
    There's no vaccine
For us to use, like spears to throw
    Against Selene!

You bring us to our knees in lust;
    Revile, demean
Us till we're ashes in the dust,
    My love, Selene!

Lamentation

Sadly, lonely,
I love thee,
Truly, only,
By this sea.

Coldly, cruelly,
You have gone,
Boldly, coolly,
Banished dawn.

Quickly, thickly
Comes my breath,
Poorly, sickly,
I'm near death.

Save me, aid me;
Salve my fear.
You have made me—
Please stay here!

Fed me, need me,
Keep me warm;
Read me, lead me
From all harm.

Bait them, hate them
Whom you trust;
Never sate them
In their lust!

Pull me, yank me
From the mire;
I will thank thee
Whole, entire.

Thou art ruthless,
I'm a fool;
Love is fruitless,
Thou art cruel!

Alchemy of Dreams

Red riots of roses run rife in my dreams
    Near the castle that shines from this hill.
The girl of my dreams, how she schemes and she schemes,
She plots and she takes me to dizzy extremes,
    She's a savage who works her own will.

I love my Cassandra who's harsher than kings,
    Though petite and as small as a child;
She is wily and anxious and yet always brings
Pure magic to dreams, and, oh, lord, how she sings!
    She's a dryad, entirely wild!

She'll strut by the west wall of gray granite made,
    Then stand with her hands on her hips.
She's elflike, amazing, a one-girl parade,
And she loves when I sing her a sad serenade
    As I bend down to kiss her sweet lips.

Her magics are potent, exceptional, drear,
    She's restless as is the sea's tide;
She wears one small opal in her tiny ear,
She is brave as a soldier and never shows fear,
    And I beg her to be my sweet bride.

She laughs when I beg and she tosses her head
    And she proffers me one tiny wrist;
Then she tells me she's made for no human's bed,
And never in dreams will she ever be wed,
    Yet allows herself to be kissed.

I awake at each dawn, but I wait for the tusk
    Of the moon that will shine most supreme;
It's in dreams where I taste and scent her sweet musk:
She greets me as always, both coyly and brusque,
    For I have no life but this dream.

Red riots of roses run rife in my dreams
    Near the castle that shines from this hill.
The girl of my dreams, how she schemes and she schemes,
She plots and she takes me to dizzy extremes,
    She's a savage who works her own will.

The Lover Despairs

I kiss thy lip,
I kiss thy ear:
Just one more sip
To conquer fear!
I kiss thy neck,
Then gasp for air—
Just one more peck
At your black hair.
To touch thy cheek,
To love thee so,
Is all I seek,
Is all I know!
I kiss thy hand
And weep for joy;
At thy command

I am thy toy.
Oh, kiss me back,
Do not refrain,
Your love I lack,
And I'm in pain.
I kiss thy lips
And kiss thy chin;
My virtue slips,
Yet it's no sin.
Ah, please be mine,
I now entreat:
Thou art so fine,
Whole and complete!
And yet you frown
And ask for proof,
And call me clown,
Remain aloof!

Duplicity

Would that my roving eye might sever
This love that withers ere it die,
And yet it is no blade can sever
A love well forged, though half a lie.
No roving eye, nor knife may sever
What God has made beneath the sky.

My fickle lover, I will stall her,
For lesser apples of mine eye!

Let her paramour now call her:
Her love for me's gone arid, dry.
Yet in the end it's I who call her,
To beg her love before I die!

The Girl

Gold on the girl whose legs are long,
    Pale jewels in her tiny ears;
Pretty she is as a winter's dawn,
    Heedless of strong men's leers.
Black is her hair that mocks the dark;
    Slim as a goddess is.
A lovely vessel, a pure pale ark,
    Revealing her bodice is.
Smiles like a Siren on her shore,
    And smile she does at me:
For I am her secret paramour,
    Here by this haunted sea.

I Dream of Her

I dream of her silver scepter,
    And a girl with shapely thighs,
And the love that bought and kept her
    In her sad, lost paradise.
Her love was a love made holy,
    As sure as the red sun rose;

And yet that girl was lonely,
    Her heart with a thousand woes.
Now in this dream I will call her,
    For I have been made twice bold.
It's my hope to win and thrall her,
    With a band of tiny gold.
And, oh, how the spirits move us
    To things most remote and chaste,
And in their good time they'll prove us,
    Then I'll have her lips to taste!

Sylph

I'm struck with that fever
    That none have controlled;
That blue-eyed deceiver
    Is finer than gold.

Her heart's like to leather,
    Her flesh is so soft;
I'm chained to her tether
    As she casts me off!

A sprite and a charmer,
    A sylph and a fay,
No man may disarm her,
    Although I yet pray.

Both flighty and airy,
    Her scent is divine;
Too late I grew wary
    Of kisses like wine.

Her kisses like butter
    That melts on your lips;
You writhe and you shudder,
    Until your heart skips.

Both nubile and supple,
    And full of such zest,
I thought us a couple;
    Now pain fills my chest.

A passionate player,
    A fraud and a thief,
My hair's turned much grayer,
    I'm wounded by grief!

No scruples, no morals,
    A girl that's twice loose,
She badgers and quarrels
    And pulls on my noose!

Her heart is like granite
    That no man may scathe,
From some distant planet,
    From some Cyclops' cave!

A strumpet, a walker
    Near brothels at dusk,
A man-eating stalker,
    With scents of strong musk.

Her ears holding jewels
    That shine like the moon;
A lure for us fools
    That she can dragoon.

An elf and a starlet,
    Pale nymph from the lake,
Some heartless cold harlot,
    Twice poisonous snake!

Like Queen Mab

So like a raptor
    Sleek and fair,
My lovely captor,
    Long soft hair;
Most wan and fragile
    Grim and coy,
Twice limber, agile,
    Snared this boy.

Both lean and wistful,
    I will grab
Her hair, a fistful,
    My Queen Mab!

Smooth and buttered,
    Like a charm,
"My love!" I uttered,
    Arm in arm.

My dreams I've numbered
    Long and slow;
Sad years I've slumbered
    Few can know.
Twice quick and graceful,
    I know this:
Her kisses tasteful,
    Kiss and kiss!

So like a raptor
    Sleek and fair,
My lovely captor,
    Long soft hair;
Most wan and fragile
    Grim and coy,
Twice limber, agile,
    Snared this boy.

The Awful Dream

In dreams of lust I thought her,
Through slave marts there I sought her,
I found her then and bought her,
    A brand behind her ear.

Away to my dark castle,
Where I am lord and vassal,
She proved to be no hassle:
    I kept her always near.

I knew but would not lend her;
I swore I would defend her;
I tried my best to mend her;
    Her hurts were most severe.
I coaxed and coached and wooed her,
And like a beau pursued her;
True love would then elude her:
    She was to me most dear.

Some dawns she'd waken crying,
And gasp with fitful sighing,
With all my love applying,
    Yet she was full of woe.
I said she'd be betraying,
That she must now be staying;
I hoped, in secret, praying,
    That she would stay, not go.

I woke one winter frightened,
The leas outside had whitened;
My heart in pain had tightened,
    My love now, she was gone.
Then all my useless trying,
Here left me hurting, dying,
Filled with a ceaseless sighing,
    I'd never see the dawn.

In dreams of lust I thought her,
Through slave marts there I sought her,
I found her then and bought her,
    A brand behind her ear.
Away to my dark castle,
Where I am lord and vassal,
She proved to be no hassle:
    I kept her always near.

Ghost Wife

Through upland and moorland I move with the mist
    And my lovers will all meet me there.
I'm pale and quite lovely right down to my wrist
That is avidly, fiercely, and tenderly kissed
    By my lovers who float on the air.

I move through the shadows, the wood and the hedge,
    And over the witch-haunted stream.
We will come to its waters, yet stop at the edge,
And my pale feet will move through the wet loamy sedge,
    Where it always appears as some dream.

My lovers are soldiers and rugged dragoons
    Who rise in the dusk from the fen.
I will sing them sweet songs, they sing marshal tunes,
Beneath the progression of waxing wan moons,
    And each night we will do this again.

I am bored with a life that is really no life;
    I am merely a ghost on the breeze,
And my sighting will cause such terror and strife,
Yet once I was young and a sweet pretty wife:
    I'm long buried here under these trees.

Through upland and moorland I move with the mist
    And my lovers will all meet me there.
I'm pale and quite lovely right down to my wrist
That is avidly, fiercely and tenderly kissed
    By my lovers who float on the air.

Jocelyn

Under these clouds of summer, and a whispered madrigal,
I sense her musk as the pale moon's tusk shines light upon this wall,
And I walk this old lane lonely, up to the vanished inn
Where I hear a word like a frightened bird, the voice of Jocelyn!

Now the wind is in the branches, her perfume on the air;
It's like a spell, so sages tell, that's blown from her fragrant hair.
And her scent is warm and lovely, like an old forgotten sin;
My steps retrace now just apace to the home of Jocelyn.

Now the years I watch them falling, like leaves blown far and free;
I come once more to the old inn door where she yet waits for me.
And in this haunted evening I hear a violin:
It makes me think, as the pale stars sink, again of Jocelyn!

Under the shadows fading, each gypsy eye's a dart;
I hear her sigh as a lone wolf's cry pierces my sad old heart.
Now out of the shadows splendid, she moves there wafer-thin,
And like shed tears, the vanished years call up my Jocelyn!

Under these clouds of summer, and a whispered madrigal,
I sense her musk as the pale moon's tusk shines light upon this wall;
And I walk this old lane lonely, up to the vanished inn,
Where I hear a word like a frightened bird, the voice of Jocelyn!

Under the Pole Star

Daylight ends in the dull dusk's danger,
    Here on this headland drear and dark.
Sad is this shadowed dreary stranger
    Under the skull moon's iron arc.
This ghost sings as her long red tresses
Fall till her form with scarlet dresses;
Her words echo in ancient stresses
    Under the Pole Star's feeble spark.

Long and lank, and a gorgeous stunner,
    She stands, sings of the olden Time.
The comets flash, each rapid runner,
    Moves to her swift enchanted rhyme.
The moon glow shows her rosy blushes,
As from her eye one curl she brushes,
All the pale ghosts this eve she hushes,
    Bathed in the scents of myrrh and lime.

Pale lips move in a haunted whisper,
    Half in shadow there on the moor.
Heart there is in this ghostly sister,
    A long-forgotten paramour.
I watch the moonlight as it traces
Her lovely face, a face of faces,
There as my pounding heart it races,
    For this pale girl I now adore.

Daylight ends in the dull dusk's danger,
    Here on this headland drear and dark.
Sad is this shadowed dreary stranger
    Under the skull moon's iron arc.
This ghost sings as her long red tresses
Fall till her form with scarlet dresses;
Her words echo in ancient stresses
    Under the Pole Star's feeble spark.

A Wellspring of Arcana

The Centauress

The wind blows leaves across your curving flank;
Your hooves all tied with ribbons purple-red,
Pure gold the hair upon your pretty head.
Your lips the perfect cup from which I drank
The strongest wine to make my mind go blank.
So it is true, exactly as you've said!
Your love can wake a stony heart long dead:
For life regained I have but you to thank.

Yet now you leave me, for you softly say
I am but one mere man, and little more;
But you, my love, you would be miles away,
Within some mythic realm upon some shore,
Where scents of myrrh and cinnamon and thyme
Have lured you back beyond all Space and Time.

One Misty Morn

One misty morn I sat
When fog hung thin and pale,
Upon the cliff top's grassy mat
And thought I saw a sail.
Rectangular that canvas flapped;
The waves seemed lavender;

This vision all my vigor sapped,
My soul began to stir.

I could not see the boat beneath,
Yet saw its silver mast.
The boat snug in a misty sheath
That sailed upon the vast.
I felt that Time had slipped apace,
That sail moved on the deep.
The mist seemed like fine tatted lace—
And then I fell asleep.

The Ale

I found myself within some ancient inn,
Perhaps three thousand years ago in Crete,
In some port town where tan girls indiscreet
Would gladly lure me to some common sin.
Mere girls they were with painted cheek and chin,
Yet I was there, I told them, but to eat
And drink, and thus old sorrows there defeat,
But gave them coins withal, for they were thin.

Then one young thing, she fetched a pewter mug
And gave it me; I watched the lathered foam.
I drank it full, that ale, and gathered years
Came flooding back, then felt an awful tug
That sought to bring me back to my lost home.
Those girls stood there, amazed at all my tears.

Daydream at Dusk

Slight silken webs of salient saffron fall
From stars stupendous on this balmy eve;
Such magic that dark wizards scarce conceive
Lights up the valley to the castle wall.
Those silken strands have wound me in their thrall,
And I am borne to realms that few perceive,
To realms so strange that I cannot believe,
Where cities on a vast plain spread and sprawl.

I'm met by girls gowned in long purple robes
Whose toe rings click across the pavement stones.
Their eyes so huge, like golden glowing globes,
They speak in song, with subtle poignant tones;
To be with them I'm moved to tears, while I
To stay with such as these would gladly die.

The Stuff of Dreams

New candle wax and canvas sails,
And girls with legs so pale and long,
With wars and darker, grim travails,
Cool mornings with a scarlet dawn,

This is the very stuff of dreams
That haunt me when the stars ascend,
Above the fields and silver streams:
They crowd me ever, without end!

Black iron gates and witches' brooms,
A rapier and falchion,
Wan ghosts that lurk above stone tombs,
And portents of oblivion;

And palaces of gold and gems,
Tall Sirens strutting down their halls,
Crowned with three-tiered brass diadems,
Who rule realms far beyond their walls.

A nubile sorceress at dusk
Who sweats within her darkling keep,
To call spells from the moon's lone tusk—
All trouble me in troubled sleep!

Sloe-eyed seductress stares at me,
I'm like some bird a snake has culled;
Above a black and haunted sea
The moon shines bright and turquoise-skulled!

A princess from an Asian isle
Has charmed me till I am undone;
So fay and gorgeous is her smile,
She leads me to oblivion!

She's limber as an athlete;
She's slim and sly, a goddess there,
With silver anklets on her feet,
And black and tempting temptress hair!

This is the very stuff of dreams
That haunts me when the stars ascend,
Above the fields and silver streams:
They crowd me ever, without end!

The Abbey Bells

"Speak low!" exclaimed one ghost,
"The abbey walls are near!"
 Her friend, he nodded thus
 As they moved from the coast
With just a tinge of fear,
 Their speech a susurrus.
 He sighed. "I know," he said,
"It is not right, or meet,
 That we, the angry dead,
 Those praying monks should greet."
"Yes, just so," she said,
"We'll here now cross these fells,
 Though we are cold and dead:
 I love the abbey's bells!"

Moonlight

Out of the dark morasses
In the night of a dwindling June,
I see the black teeming masses
By the light of low-slung moon.

Like adders with red-tongued hisses
Playing some dissonant tune,
Or Sirens with dripping kisses
Who swarm by the glow of the moon,

Near the great gray cairn on the headland,
At the cry of a high soaring loon,
Can be seen this arid and dead land
In the lurid light of the moon.

Out of the dark morasses
There is chanted an ancient rune,
And so age on swift age passes
Under the light of the moon.

Vespers

I took the weed-strewn path, the steep ascent,
Up to the ruin where the mouse and hare
Gambol where once Franciscans knelt in prayer,
Prepared for Christmas or the weeks in Lent.
Discalced would they walk, their shaved heads bent,
Through orchards in these fields where peach and pear
Ripened in the sun, scenting all the air,
Their quiet lives most steadfast, still, content.

I sat against a ruined wall; the place
Was hung with ivy in a great festoon
That seemed to lend this shell an added grace

At noon time or beneath an opal moon,
While I a strong desire sought to quell
And strained to hear the ghostly vesper bell.

Time and Space

Over gibbets, under eyes,
Over gibbets, under skies,
Over gallows, underground,
There at dusk pale ghosts abound.

At the thunder, at the lane,
At the thunder, at the rain,
At the thunder spirits come,
Thunder's like a mighty drum.

Past the graveyard, there's the spruce,
Past the graveyard, there's the noose,
Past the graveyard, rung on rung,
There the ghostly men are hung.

From the stars and from the lane,
From the stars and from the slain,
From the stars, out of the Past,
Time and Space stretch ever vast.

Spoons

I dreamed one night of metal spoons,
Of gold and silver and of tin,
Some huge and lethal like harpoons,
Some tiny, elegant, and thin.

Some used to stir strong anodynes
By wizards on cold Martian moons,
With slender, rounded, triple tines,
Bone handles on these mantic spoons.

I saw one titan, gleaming spoon
That roiled the inlets and the bays,
Then whorled into a great typhoon,
That lasted for a hundred days!

Some temptress-shaped with sleek legs bare,
These loveliest of silver spoons,
And solid gold all their long hair,
Pale eyes like dreamy afternoons.

I dreamed one night of metal spoons,
Of gold and silver and of tin,
Some huge and lethal like harpoons,
Some tiny, elegant, and thin.

The Sunken Road

The sunken road when winter stalks,
A place where storm winds whip, erode,
A place a rider stops and balks,
    The sunken road.

Long ago a curse bestowed
Upon this road in idle talk;
At nightfall is a pointed goad.

By night they say a dark loon mocks
All riders where the bent oak's bowed.
That's why no living being walks
    The sunken road.

New Love for Old

I am the Shadow's voice who cries:
"I sell new love for old!"
  There, in your dreams, I hear your sighs.
"I sell new love for gold!"

Yet if no gold you have, then I
Will save you from despair:
I'll take old love and then I'll fly,
Weave new love from the air!

I will make him, or will make her
Like gods long lost to Time;
Such lust and love will they then stir,
New love that is sublime!

I am the Shadow's voice who cries:
"I sell new love for old!"
  There, in your dreams, I hear your sighs.
"I kill old loves for gold!"

Isfahan

To Isfahan I watch them flow,
Each long and winding caravan,
From deserts to the far plateau,
    To Isfahan.

With silver, gold and harlots tan,
Whose eyes with visions overflow
With magics that the ages span.

In dreams I see this strange tableau
Not seen by any other man.
Ever I watch the camels go
    To Isfahan.

Remembrance

Remember when those clay brick walls
Stood tall, just one mile from the fen,
And all the bluejays' strident calls—
    Remember when?

And how the old lane in the glen
Filled up with young girls' madrigals,
Mixed with the magpie and the wren?

Yet now each twisted shadow falls
Against that wall time and again.
I whisper, one who still recalls,
    "Remember when?"

Serenity

Serenity eludes my grasp.
The golden ring seems not for me,
Still for it I yet strain and gasp:
    Serenity.

I've spanned this far-flung galaxy;
I thirst for it, I cough and rasp,
And cast dark spells of sorcery.

I've broken every iron hasp
On books of black necromancy,
Yet vainly I still seek to clasp
    Serenity.

Scryer

I scry the glass when shadows flee.
The idol with its feet of brass
Tilts in the farmstead's misty lea.
    I scry the glass.

A likely lad or winsome lass
Picks asters there so happily,
While untold eons pile and pass.

And far away is heard the sea
While silent footfalls in the grass
Awaken sorrows deep in me.
    I scry the glass.

The Glory Hand

The mist was like some cloying smoke,
The frozen fen like cured concrete;
A frozen hand profaned the peat
And seemed to beckon to the oak.
Some conjured spell it then awoke.

Now I marked well the glory hand
That rose from out that frozen fen,
That seemed an evil guardian
No cryptic magic might withstand
Within this place or any land.

Then all the evening's misty gloom
Fell twice as heavy as before.
I strode as down some corridor
To seek some scented lover's room,
My roiling heart a dark simoom.

The earth, my heart, were frozen hard
Like icy moons that, spinning, ride
Mars' orbit and the stars bestride.
The swamp oaks each a silent guard
Would not my tears the least regard.

The mist was like some cloying smoke,
The frozen fen like cured concrete.
A frozen hand profaned the peat
And seemed to beckon to the oak.
Some conjured spell it then awoke.

The Old Shop

I spied the alabaster horse
In dust upon a cedar shelf.
There in between a cast bronze elf
And knife whose origin was Norse.

Each polished eye a dull red stone,
Its tail snapped off so long ago;
Its surface like to dirty snow,
This beast of antique carven bone.

And then it seemed some sorcerer
Came through the curtain in surprise;
Red-robed he stood with feral eyes,
The old shop's stooped proprietor.

Between us not the least discourse,
But yet I heard a silent sigh.
The sun was blocked, a darkened sky
Then filled me with a nameless force.

The years have passed and now atop
My oak-hewn mantel sits that horse.
So strange to think that still, perforce,
I cannot find that ancient shop!

Winter Spells

On white serrated peaks where mist accrues,
I come when winter stalls this land with ice.
Titanic winds these landscapes chop and dice,
Where ice sheets crown these heights in mystic blues.
And winter will, with spells, this realm infuse,
Where death may take the heedless in a trice,
The snow queen, still alluring, will entice
The hapless man that she may deem to choose.

And I am one she claimed in ages Past.
I wait for winter near her hidden throne;
Her realm this winter is extreme and vast,

A wan rare beauty, with a heart like stone.
So when these mighty winds like thunders drum
She speaks to you, alone, and bids thee come!

Girl with a Crystal Ball

I sit here at my window sill,
And know the crystal does not lie.
I see I walk beside the mill
With some young man ungainly, shy.

I rub the ball, again I scan
Its crystal deeps and, scanning, sigh.
I'm in the arms of that young man,
We lie together in the rye.

But then the crystal clouds and these
Bright visions are unclear. I scry
A world of dark and stormy seas;
No signs can I identify.

But then the quartz, it seems to clear!
Excited now, I'm like to die;
However, deep within the sphere
I stand alone beneath the sky.

Give Me a Brand

Give me a brand and a lyre!
Give me a steed of black!
I will ride till the stars expire
And the walls of this city crack.

Higher and higher I climb,
Each harlot a tear she'll shed.
I'll ride up the halls of Time
To sleep in a harlot's bed!

Now over these twilit dunes,
Under the orb of Mars,
I wait till these monstrous moons
Eclipse the ravening stars.

Give a brand and a lyre!
Give me a steed to fly!
I swear I will not tire
Until the day I die.

The Bell

At night I am a bell
You hear from deep inside
That summons up a spell.

Some inn or dark hotel
Is where I sometimes hide;
At night I am a bell.

Who is there might foretell
That it is love denied
That summons up a spell?

At dawn I am the shell
That's left here by the tide;
At night I am a bell.

My tale once more retell
To fan the flames of pride
That summons up a spell.

Ah, like the spawn of hell
I'm with you stride for stride!
At night I am a bell
That summons up a spell.

The Riven Oak

I took that trail as dusk fell fast
Against the incandescent hills,
And told myself the Past was past,
Though memory both thrills and chills;
Hard by the scarred and riven oak
I felt the cloying clutch of doom,
And in the air the stench of smoke—
An acrid sulfurous perfume!
Now when dusk falls again I mime
And ape my steps from out the Past;

Once more this mountain trail I climb
Below this starry ether vast.

The Rescue

Thy words most enchanting, refreshing,
    Thy hair like ripe grain,
Ere it is done with the threshing—
    Ah, love is such pain.
I will slay all thy archers in tandem
    Who hold thee at bay;
Their survivors but few and random:
    Come with me, pray?

The curve of thy neck is alluring,
    Thy beauty a sign;
So I spend all my time adoring,
    For thou, alone, art mine.
I will slay all thy foemen conniving,
    Over this misty sod,
Not one of them all surviving
    From my iron rod!

Ransom

I scour dreams in the gloaming
    Until bright jewels appear,
Then I am done with roaming,
    Placing one in thy ear.
Thou wilt hold me there in the morning
    Until you have captured me,
As these stars are less than alluring,
    For thou hast enraptured me.

Come, give me a wine of the highlands
    Poured in a cup of gold,
Or bring me arrack from the islands,
    Tart and strong and bold!
Pray, stay with me under this awning,
    For thou most hansom be;
I will spend these long years fawning
    For thou wilt ransom me!

Hammer

    I forged a hammer from the stars
In vats of molten broth that hold
    Pig iron sucked from iron bars,
And chased the haft with gleaming gold.

    And then I built fantastic realms
With double stars that nightly ride

    Like strange ships steered by stranger helms,
While solar winds stirred up the tide.

    Now with my hammer I would forge
The white cliffs round a foaming sea,
    As well as dale and vale and gorge,
And place blue flowers in the lea.

    I swung my hammer till it sang
From mountain peak down to the lawn;
    Its echoes through the valleys rang,
From dawn to splendid golden dawn.

The End of the Wizards

The heavy wooden chests were Balinese,
    Eight giant steins were all from pewter cast,
The rafters split up form a schooner's mast;
    The glowing paper lamps were all Chinese.
Here window glass imported from Belize
    By wizards whose thaumaturgy was vast,
Who lorded over all until at last
    They disappeared upon the evening breeze.

One sorceress came from the high plateau,
    Tall as an Amazon, her eyes were gray.
One look from her made all the mages go
    Like colors in a fireworks display.
She slowly swirled her long and silken sash
    And watched them fly away like wind-blown ash.

The Departure of Malygris

A Spell in Measure

I cast a spell in measure
    To bind and to trap thee;
Thou wilt obey my pleasure,
    As my spells enwrap thee.
I will drain the might of Orion,
    Hammer him with a rod;
For I am his heir and his scion,
    Like unto a god.

Thou wilt love me night and morning,
    My arms enwinding thee;
With gems thy throat adorning,
    What pleasure finding thee!
I will bind up thy wounds with a balm
    Upon this green sod;
Now under the shade of this palm,
    Sit thou with a god!

Magics

Gather the stars and the moon for a spell,
With holly and sard and an umber conch shell,
And sing to the sound of
A bell left unrung;
With a pestle-ground love
Till your song is re-sung.

Call on a harlot who's pale as the moon,
Call on her nightly, but call on her soon;
And while she is weeping,
Take one crystal tear,
And when she is sleeping
One jewel from her ear.

Gather them there near your hearth at the dawn,
Drench them with dew from the grass on the lawn;
And while it is brewing
Like some frothing sea,
You'll soon then be wooing,
But me, only me!

Winter

I watch the gray ponds harden
When winter stalks the day,
And watch the gales blow whitely,
Both daily and then nightly,
Dead flowers in my garden,
With winds blown from the bay.
I watch the gray ponds harden
When winter stalks the day.

Now stark and all asunder,
My roses lie in death
Until the warm sun, gleaming,
Once more its life is streaming

And will the winter sunder
And give us breath for breath.
Now stark and all asunder,
My roses lie in death.

Though now the king of cold is
Harsh liege of all this land,
And haply lords it over
The flowers, grasses, clover,
Until the sun's pure gold is
New liege above the strand,
Though now the king of cold is
Harsh liege of all this land.

Here right beside this willow,
Within this haunted night,
Half waking and half dreaming,
I hear the snowstorm screaming,
As wan as any billow,
And deathly, deathly white.
Here right outside my window,
Within this haunted night!

Then out upon the headland
I hear the breakers roll
Where titan waves are crashing,
Ghost ships yet listing, thrashing;
Across this icy dead land
I hear the bronze bell toll.
Then out upon the headland
I hear the breakers roll.

And then at freezing midnight
I see the ghost of spring
That comes the winter after
With love and lovers' laughter
And where all the world seems light.
Here joyous bells will ring,
And then at freezing midnight
I see the ghost of spring.

This storm so like a river
That rages to the sea;
That howls like grey wolves stalking,
Like goblins laughing, talking,
Until I quiver, shiver,
In my extremity.
This storm so like a river
That rages to the sea.

I spy the storm winds veering
Across the Channel Isles;
There where the dead are sleeping,
Their secrets guarding, keeping,
As out there in the clearing
The ruined peristyles.
I spy the storm winds veering
Across the Channel Isles.

I watch the gray ponds harden
When winter stalks the day,
And watch the gales blow whitely,

Both daily and then nightly,
Dead flowers in my garden,
With winds blown from the bay.
I watch the gray ponds harden
When winter stalks the day.

Harpies and Ravens

Harpies and ravens pull stitching and seams,
And harry and haunt all night in my dreams
As over the barrows
On these cold dreary coasts
I flee silver arrows
From bow shots of ghosts.

Shadows now stretching to hills where they strain,
To tombs of dead kings whose cairns still enchain.
Here you'll find roaming
Dark liches of eld
Who rise in the gloaming
By magics propelled.

Yet waking or sleeping I still cannot tell
If such things are proper or base and most fell
For harpies are evil
And ravens but caw,
Such things seem medieval
While obeying no law.

Love Is Cruel

Swiftly sever
    All our love,
Ban it ever
    All thereof.
Throw it over
    Far and far;
Burn my lover
    In a star!

Sweep the ashes
    In the sea!
Ninety lashes,
    Come scourge me!
Love's cold dart
    Struck me, a fool,
And broke my heart.
    Love is cruel.

The Pond

I will go down to that haunted pond
    Under a midnight sky,
And I'll fetch me there one hazel wand
    And I'll use it bye and bye.
Ah, yes, it was death that broke our bond,
    Deep in this pond you lie.

I will go down, and none may stall me,
    And none may stay my hand,
For it was here that she would call me
    Out of a far strange land;
And in her arms beguile and thrall me,
    Her wish then my command.

Lover of the Moon

I took the moon to wife by this cold stream.
Her silver kisses soothed me while her hair
Of gossamer, it floated on the air;
Her flesh was like to milk and rosy cream,
Her love the stuff of nightmare and of dream.
I fell asleep and so she left me there,
A broken man, a slave to black despair,
For I was snared within her clever scheme.

And now each day I come here with the dusk
And cannot wait to see her here arise,
To dream once more of her enchanting musk.
Yet as I do salt tears come to my eyes:
I am a lover broken, spent and torn,
A wayfarer who's utterly forlorn.

A Ghost

I shushed a ghost.
She whispered low.
"I'm from the coast,"
She said.
She floated there
Exceeding slow,
With scarlet hair,
One hundred years long dead.

"I seek a kiss,"
She told me then.
This pretty miss,
A snare to men,
Yet now a ghost.
I smiled. We kissed,
And she went back then
To the coast.

Ghost in the Mirror

    In the mirror on my dresser
    I can see the dead transgressor
As she smiles within the surface of the oily, glassy lake.
    Now I am the sole possessor
    Of the mirror on my dresser,
Yet though I've hammered and I've battered this glass it will not break.

    She was once my sweet caresser
    How I tried to own, possess her,
But she fooled me and she fueled me like a coiling blue-eyed snake.
    While I always tried to bless her,
    It all somehow seemed to stress her,
So I slew her in the reeds one dusk down in the muddy brake.

    Now her ghost is her successor.
    I no longer can distress her—
Now she haunts me in the night every moment I'm awake!
    Now I cannot stall, suppress her,
    My tall ghostly mad aggressor,
As she drags me through the garden and she drowns me in the lake.

    In the mirror on my dresser,
    She is now the sole possessor,
For my ghost it wanders dreadful in the cold and turbid lake.
    Now at midnight on my dresser,
    All the starlight will fluoresce her,
Until that house will crumble and that twice awful mirror break!

Wind-Blown Dream

Wind-blown dream of the brothel calling,
    There in the twilight, in the gloom,
Here where all lust is most appalling
    There in that designated room;
Here where a young girl's entertained me,

Here where my own sin's ever stained me,
Here where the passions locked and chained me,
    Deep in this dream like to a tomb.

Give the gold that the gilt girls covet,
    Stamped in the mints hard by the mine.
They toil at dusk, the gold they love it,
    The gold and silver fine, all fine.
Love is a thing of which they're wary,
Their hearts and souls each dusk they bury,
So many men, yet none to marry:
    They think of men as Circe's swine.

The Dusk

The dusk falls quick as the red sun sets,
Long shadows cast as odd silhouettes
    Are framed as the gold red sun goes down
    In twilight tints of a soft red brown,
And I'm left alone with remorse and regrets
    Beyond the edge of this ancient town,
Where the white oaks stand like statuettes.
    Here the wind in a rush whips up this sea,
    Where the owls and the nightjars flit and flee.

My love once a bird in a silver cage,
Now so long gone, dark age on age,
    Where I wrapped her in arms of love like gold
    To keep her from harm and the dark world's cold.

She but a child, while I was a mage,
    Yet I scoffed at all the world foretold,
And her loss no power might assuage,
    Here the wind in a rush whips up this sea,
    Where the owls and the nightjars flit and flee.

The Glue

I watched a red and mean mendacious Mars,
Its orbitings through clouds of ormolu;
Then set my conjurings with spells from Katmandu.
My brazier flamed, its smoke of cinnabars,
And rose in steely spools toward signal stars,
Until it seemed the all too human glue
Of sanity came loose, and I was due
To fall upon a thousand scimitars!

I shut my book of spells, but then too late,
For coming down a ladder from the moon
A horde of avatars sprang through my gate,
Each ugly as a prancing mad baboon,
To climb my stairs and rip me then to shreds:
Like so much cloth they tore apart my threads.

The Haunted Clock

The clock was made from polished brass and teak.
Some thought it magical. It was quite old,

And many claimed strong spirits long patrolled
The mantel where it sat, this strange antique.
Some thought it Swiss, while others thought it Greek.
Its brazen bell at midnights only tolled;
Its hands were iron, worked with yellow gold;
It was a piece arcane, and most unique.

One night I woke and stumbled down the stair;
The clock had called me hither in a dream,
Though it was May, so bitter cold the air.
Struck by moonlight in one long silver stream,
I marveled at its cunning and its craft,
And then I screamed! I swear that it had laughed!

Nocturnal

Near the cold queued cairns where the ghosts croon suing
    Lost lovers who lure them all under this moon,
They float and flutter, weave webs with their wooing,
    And frighten a fleeing lost little loon.
In their gossamer gowns these ghosts strut alluring
    Those men of the past standing stalwart as trees,
Their splendid dead heroes were once so adoring,
    Now float on the breeze.

The night's narcissistic, wan women wistful,
    Anoint their cool flesh with fragrant aloes,
They hold in cold hands, each tiny fistful
    Of rose petals flung here pale as the rose.

Though deep in their tombs, their bones sere and broken,
    They rise up at dusk from each stony bed,
Each leaves at her cairn one rose as a token,
    There for the dead.

Past hills where the winds ruffle pale purple grasses
    These women will soar with birds of the air;
Over tall oaks and down through the passes,
    They fly with their ghostly and long streaming hair.
Over the arch of a tower that's tumbled
    Down to its granite and pale pitted pave
They hover in silence, abashed and humbled,
    As over a grave.

The winds from the south call out with their screaming,
    To awaken these women here under the stars;
Their ghosts now assemble and think they are dreaming,
    The moon in its phases like pale scimitars.
Under the eye of Orion they wander:
    "What strange place is this?" they whisper as one.
They mark unknown spires that rise over yonder,
    The night then is done.

Of Fairy Rings and Cedar Chests

I dreamed of fairy rings and cedar chests,
Of starry headlands where the green sea foams,
Of Caesar and the binding might of Rome,
Of pterosaurs with plumed and pastel crests.

And, too, I've dreamed of tawny midnight guests
Who rose from out the quicksand and the loam,
Who moved like spirits in my humble home,
Each dawn returning to their earthy nests.

Then in one dream I woke upon some isle,
Remote and lonely with an icy chill;
With none there to bemuse, bewitch, beguile,
The sea grew calm, and it is ever still.
And now each dawn I wake, and I am there,
Beyond all death and love, there's just despair.

The Woodland Nymph

Lush is life on this lakeside laving
    Her long lean legs at breaking dawn;
This nymph who knows no life of slaving,
    Moved by the spirit, then is gone.
Here in the wild wood, supple, clever,
Her goal, men's hearts to break and sever;
Free is this nymph both now and ever,
    A pretty girl, exceeding wan.

Old she is as the dream of Time is,
    Seems but a child, or scarce a teen;
To live for love to her no crime is,
    For some new beau is she most keen.
There in the shadows resting, sleeping,
With those same shadows restless, creeping,

Across these woods where magic's keeping
    Her beauty young, her eyes deep green.

I watch her from my restless cover,
    Over the hillock's thick dark fern,
Dream of her as a precious lover,
    And for such love I nightly burn!
In dreams, alone, I deftly hover
Over this nymph and just above her—
Oh, with such passion how I loved her!
    I fear she is both coy and stern.

Then one dawn in the thin air spying,
    She came to me all unaware;
There where I lay both sad and sighing,
    She let me touch her lovely hair.
Then such a thrill no mortal savors,
Then a kiss with fantastic flavors,
Then would I learn unheard-of favors—
    I choked and gasped to take in air!

Now in my sleep I'm ever scheming
    To find once more that lovely thing;
Only within the realm of dreaming
    My soul will soar, a bird on the wing!
She is a will-o'-the-wisp adorning
All of my dreams till the light of morning,
And ever my heart and soul suborning;
    Remembered loves such sorrows bring.

Pursued by the Jinn

I dreamt an evil jinn pursued me there
Across the sultan's vast and desert lands.
Knowing full well my life he now demands,
He has electrified the very air!
And yet I fool him at each turn. No snare
He sets for me works now on any strands,
And while he has, if need be, many hands,
Of all his schemings I seem most aware.

And then one day a nubile girl, and pale,
Sat weeping by a dreary little lane.
I answered back her small and plaintive hail,
She hugged my knees and wept like summer rain.
Then she grew tall; her eyes were brilliant greens:
She hammered me to splintered smithereens.

The Gander

I dream of old lovers
    Bereft and forlorn;
Their memory smothers
    And pricks like a thorn.

In castles sequestered
    On some haunted hill,
Such lovers I've pestered
    And pester them still.

A rake and betrayer,
  I'm king of the con,
Abuse and delay her
  Like any Don Juan.

I'm harsh as is granite
  Right here from the start;
From planet to planet
  I'll break a girl's heart.

A rogue and a miser,
  A poisonous snake,
I'll use and despise her
  Like any mean rake.

But then in one city
  I'll never forget,
For more is the pity,
  I learned of regret!

So small and alluring,
  Green eyes like the sea,
She flirted, suborning
  The roué in me!

Like Herod's young daughter,
  She led me, a lamb,
And ripe for the slaughter,
  Most forlorn I am!

She seduced and she tempted,

    I thought I owned her;
I was not exempted,
    My mind's half a blur.

The love that I gave her
    Was true as could be;
I sought then to save her
    When *she* betrayed *me!*

I weep when the summer
    Still blooms on the hill,
That merciless drummer
    Of pain with me still!

I long now to savor
    Those sweet lips once pure,
While the love that I gave her
    Rots here on this shore!

I dream of old lovers
    Bereft and forlorn;
Their memory smothers
    And pricks like a thorn.

An Elixir of Love

One lizard's eye,
A lark's light feather,
A lover's sigh,
One magic tether

In my potion
I slowly spill:
This tiny ocean
To work my will!

One drop of wine
That drops therein;
Some secret sign,
A harlot's sin.
A lover's kiss,
Some hag's dark curse,
Just this and this,
And nothing worse.

The Ghostly Monarch

I gathered legions slowly in the West
With all the far horizons glimmering;
The opalescent moon there shimmering,
As scouting harpies now will sure attest.
My concubines once more their love professed
And kissed mine opal silver signet ring,
As lines of weaving slaves would to me bring
Glass urns of gems brought in at my request.

My teeming cohorts, rank on rank, they swelled,
And trumpeters would echo on the marge.
I watched subalterns as they pranced and yelled,
With everything made ready for the charge.

I stood, unsheathed my golden sword right there,
And so it was we vanished in the air.

The Forsaken City

In cities forsaken,
    In deserts grown sere,
At dawn I awaken,
    At dawn I appear!

These stone columns fluted,
    All cracked and they tilt;
This ghost city's muted,
    And never rebuilt.

I move through its alleys
    Long drifted with sand;
These stars like strange galleys
    That none may command.

Near mall and bordello
    The old stage is set;
Its stones have turned yellow,
    Its ghosts know regret.

I once knew a slattern,
    Both comely and sweet,
That sad daily pattern
    Of girls of the street.

Both lovely and graceful
    And kind as a child,
Was always most tasteful
    And yet could be wild.

For years I would meet her
    Out under these stars;
I'd kiss her then greet her—
    Ah, such love was ours.

Yet sad was the dawning
    That struck like a knife,
When under this awning
    She ended her life.

The night wind still whispers,
    The brothel is gone;
And so are her sisters,
    To oblivion.

Through cities forsaken
    By eagle and kite,
With regret am I taken
    And weep through the night.

The Moon Riders

Down in the valley,
    Down in the dell,
Sad spirits sally
    Out on the fell.

It's here I count them,
    Lonely and cold,
Ghost horses, mount them,
    Saddles of gold.

Out to the heather,
    Out to the moors,
Inclement weather,
    Snow-covered shores.
Horsemen so pale as
    Sea foam at dawn,
Ghostly and frail as
    Dew on the lawn.

Ride through the woodland,
    Down by the dale,
Bad land or good land,
    Oh, how they sail!
Ever resourceful,
    Both near and far,
Sad and remorseful,
    Under some star.

Under Orion,
    Hard by the sea,
Horsemen yet fly on
    Most gallantly!
Ever outsiders,
    March or in June,
Gallop these riders
    Under the moon.

I Remember

Do you recall the fire, hearth, and the cold,
And each splendid glowing ember,
All glowing there like glowing gold?
Do you remember?

Do you recall God's grace in that winter,
And too the ghost of September,
Lines of frost the window pane would splinter?
Do you not remember?

What of your warm kisses under the eaves,
The snow in an icy sprawl?
And still I see your pale and silken sleeves—
These things I well recall.

Do you recall the fire, the hearth's hot breath,
Yes, heat from each white-gold ember,
How they flamed out, went down to death,
Like thee? Yes, I remember.

With a Vengeance

I dreamed a woman rode the palest horse:
His name was Death, and vengeance was their trade;
And through the city's streets, on a crusade,
She'd hand out justice with an awful force.

Her being stemmed from some old nameless source,
While evil men thought her some mad charade;
Yet Death rode under silks and fine brocade—
Her targets perished there without recourse.

I met her one dark night out in the lea;
She stood beside her steed and eyed me there.
Some opiate then so affected me,
The scent from lovely, black and lavish hair.
I grew helpless, with nothing I could do.
She said: "This night, good sir, I've come for you!"

Wizard

I mumbled spells high in my castle keep.
Some iron wind blew half the stars away;
They flamed out in a most bizarre display,
Then sizzled in the far and vasty deep.
And then a rising tide came in to sweep
This headland and these cliffs into the bay.
Both earth and moon were stalled, and they
Charmed all this realm to strange eternal sleep.

And then I fumbled with a glass carafe
To watch the stars remaining then align.
I squeezed most tightly on my magic staff,
Then poured and drank this incandescent wine.
Though I was mad, yet successful in my scheme
To turn this world into a waking dream.

Men

I heard the lyre singing
    From grottos in the shade
As turtledoves went winging
    To love nests they had made.
The scent of love now floated
    In ways obtuse and rare,
From pale nymphs golden-throated
    And traveled on the air.

The sleeping fauns still lazy,
    Those nymphs sang past the fen,
As dusk grew thick and hazy
    To reach the world of men.
I heard their magic cooing
    That set those nymphs apart;
They sought for human wooing
    And charmed my broken heart!

I traveled through the rushes,
    Their words a sweet aloe.
Their love, they say, it hushes
    All thought of pain and woe.
They met me in the clearing
    And placed a rose festoon
Around my neck, endearing,
    These daughters of the moon.

We frolicked in the grasses
    And laughed across the dell.
Here Time so quickly passes,
    As dawn light broke the spell.
I begged the girls to tarry
    And kiss me once again.
I offered them to marry,
    They laughed and whispered, "men!"

I heard the lyre singing
    From grottos in the shade
As turtledoves went winging
    To love nests they had made.
The scent of love now floated
    In ways obtuse and rare,
From pale nymphs golden-throated
    And traveled on the air.

The Harpy Queen

Floating castles,
Scented hair,
Ghostly vassals
Ride the air,
Pale princesses
Wan as rice
Wear incenses
Of sweet spice.

Harpies soaring
In this sky,
Oceans roaring
Just nearby,
Like an eagle
She will rise,
Slim and regal
From these skies.

Wings of leather,
Eyes of green,
Mystic treasure
Harpy queen;
Pretty flyer,
Predator,
Wicked, dire,
On this shore.

Lovers taken
To her lair,
Frighten, shaken,
Gasp for air.
Lonely hours
There alone,
She devours
Flesh and bone!

A Fragment from a Dream*

If I were what the rose is
And you, my love, were dew,
I'd scent you with sweet fragrance,
Sing songs of heartfelt cadence
More precious than red roses
On paths that angels knew.
If I were what the rose is
And you, my love, were dew.

*I "composed" this in a few seconds in a dream in the early morning hours of November 3, 2007. I realized that if I did not get up and write it down it would be irretrievably lost forever. I have changed only one word of it: the first word of line 4 from "And" to "Sing" . . .

I Dream

I dream of love, a castle,
    And magic as of old,
A princess and a vassal,
    And gods of hammered gold;

Of scented hair, and longing,
    And caves of deep-gouged ice,
Of spirits pale and thronging
    The walls of Paradise!

Of rivers cold and scarlet,
    And loves betrayed for naught,

Of one petite young harlot
    Whom my poor heart has caught!

Of castles in the canyons
    Beyond some haunted stream,
Of huge and ancient banyans
    That grow in deepest dream;

Of pennants blue and regal
    That flew from ramparts high,
Where soars the hawk and eagle,
    Above them in the sky.

Of gangly girls whose laughter
    Echoed cleanly there,
As hidden in the rafter
    I watched them unaware;

Of forts with massive walling
    And splendid masonry,
Yet now decrepit, falling
    Into an angry sea.

Of camels plodding quickly
    On routes unknown to man,
And sandstorms blowing thickly
    Against that caravan;

Of sleepy kings half snoring,
    Who owned lost diamond mines,

Attended by adoring
    Svelte gray-eyed concubines.

I dream of galleys rowing
    Where wafts a salty breeze,
Of mighty storm winds blowing
    Beyond the Hebrides.

I dream of armies routed
    In deserts drear and tan,
And love that's never doubted
    In mythic Isfahan.

I dream of carnal pleasures
    In alleyways of sin,
And magics no man measures
    Once woven by the jinn.

I dream that love disposes
    Base evil and its ilk,
Till all that's left are roses
    And gowns of pretty silk.

On nights when I am lonely
    Hard by this midnight sea,
The single cure is only
    That you are here with me.

A Ghost Girl from 1918

A ghost I circle here above
The old street where I once would walk,
Where I once sold to all my love,
A pretty girl as pale as chalk.

The soldiers loved me in the heat,
Or when the winter storms would come;
I wished them well, their foe defeat,
As they marched off to fife and drum.

Just made enough so I'd get by;
I worked in Paris with my friends.
Sometimes, alone, at night I'd cry,
And worked in Nantes and Amiens.

The war dragged on for bitter years;
We made less money in that time.
At Christmas I'd cry bitter tears,
And work for nothing half the time.

We saw few men. Each was a boy,
Afraid of death, yet full of boast.
I took one home, filled him with joy;
On Christmas Day I made him toast.

Then in the last year of the war,
One soldier he would strangle me.
He had his way, then called me "whore,"
And killed me just to save his fee.

A ghost I circle here above
The old street where I once would walk,
Where I once sold to all my love,
A pretty girl as pale as chalk.

The Caliph's Lover

Near inland rivers ghosts awaken,
    There under marshal moons grown cold;
I visit there, my soul so shaken,
    And mark huge columns flecked with gold.
One regal spirit tall and stately,
She speaks to say strange realms await me,
And by that God who did create me,
    She is most beautiful and bold!

She takes me to lost Perelandra,
    Then to the ziggurat of Ur,
Then too the oracle Cassandra
    Upon that dismal Trojan shore.
Unto lost realms so cold, benighted,
To madmen all of hell's excited,
To lovely women scorned and slighted,
    She left me in lost Rajapore.

Then wandering far in Rajapore,
    Heard tintinnabulations there,
Come from the caliph's paramour,
    With small bells woven in her hair!

And like a magnet was drawn to her,
And loving her I sought to woo her,
I looked again and knew I knew her:
    She was a goddess of the air!

She swept me to the clouds of morning,
    Below a soft tranquility;
Loved me, all her old lovers scorning,
    Hard by that aqua-tinted sea!
My heart like horses wildly racing,
Untold blisses dreaming, tracing,
All my old dreams fast erasing,
    I stood upon eternity!

Pursuit of the Belovèd

She has cast off my love like some sari,
    To flee like a doe in the dark;
She is only and ever my quarry,
    Under the high heavens' arc.
I pursue with a will and an ardor
    Under translucent night skies;
She will find no homeland or harbor,
    For she is my prize!

I've laid siege this day to her castle
    By strong legions patrolled,
Yet soon I will be her proud vassal
    And take all her love and her gold.

Her legions I'll harry, annoy them,
    Disperse them both shod and unshod,
Their remnants crush and destroy them
    With my iron rod.

www.ingramcontent.com/pod-product-compliance
Lightning Source LLC
Chambersburg PA
CBHW070959160426
43193CB00012B/1843